NOTICE OF PARISH

PARISH OF HADLEIGH

NOTICE IS HEREBY GIVEN that a PARISH MEETING for the above-named Parish will be held at the COUNCIL SCHOOLS, on **Monday, the 5th day of December, 1927,** at 8 o'clock in the Evening.

The Business to be transacted will be as follows :

To determine the adoption of the following recommendations of the Parish Council :—

A. That the best interests of Local Government of the Parish would be served by the amalgamation of Hadleigh and the County Borough of Southend-on-Sea provided that the initial rating should be satisfactorily adjusted, and that the Parish Council be authorised to negotiate in that behalf should an opportunity recur before March 31st next.

B. In default of such an opportunity the Parish Council recommend :—

(1) That application be made to the Local Government Committee of the County Council for the creation of an Urban District consisting of Hadleigh and so much of Thundersley and Eastwood as may be included within a drainage area falling to the East.

(2). Alternatively that the Parish Council be instructed further to negotiate with South Benfleet, with a view to the formation of a combined Urban District, but not to consent to joining therein until the parishioners in statutory meeting assembled shall give consent to the result of further consideration.

(3). That it is undesirable at the present time to include with Hadleigh the Western and North-Western portions of the Parish of Thundersley.

Such Persons only will be entitled to attend as are registered as Local Government Electors in the Parish.

Dated this 19th day of November, 1927.

D. H. Stibbards

{ *Chairman of the Parish Council.*

Notice of Parish Meeting, 1927. (Reproduced by courtesy of Castle Point Borough Council.)

HADLEIGH PAST

Hadleigh church *c*.1915, showing the north side before the vestry was built.

HADLEIGH PAST

Ian Yearsley

Best wishes

Ian Yearsley

Christmas 1998

Phillimore

1998

Published by
PHILLIMORE & CO. LTD.
Shopwyke Manor Barn, Chichester, West Sussex

ISBN 1 86077 078 9

Printed and bound in Great Britain by
BIDDLES LTD.
Guildford, Surrey

This book is dedicated to my parents

Contents

List of Illustrations

Frontispiece: Hadleigh Church *c.*1915, showing the north side before the vestry was built.

Acknowledgements

The illustrations in this book are reproduced by courtesy of the following: Derek Barber, 19, 29, 32, 38, 40-1, 49, 52, 56, 63, 66, 69-70, 78, 80-1, 89-93, 96, 98-9, 102-3, 105, 109, 111-2, 115, 121-2, 124, 130-1, 133-4, 138-9, 141-6, 148, 151; British Library, 14; Castle Point Borough Council, 101, 126; Edward Clack, 2, 13; Colchester Museums, 1, 7; Bob Delderfield, 31, 35-6, 43-4, 46, 53, 55, 57-8, 61, 106-7, 129; P.L. Drewett, 22-3; English Heritage, 15; Essex County Council, 163; Essex Record Office, 16-8, 20, 28, 33, 48, 59, 65, 71-2, 82-3, 85, 87, 116-7, 119-20, 137, 149-150; S. Moss, 132; Phillimore & Co Ltd, 25; Sheila Pitt-Stanley, 50; Salvation Army International Heritage Centre, 34, 64, 67, 73, 77, 100; Southend Borough Council, 140; Southend Library, 60, 74, 86, 147; Southend Museums Service, 24, 27, 54, 88, 108, 110, 114, 123, 125, 127, 135-6. All other pictures are from the author's collection.

Apart from the purely numerical acknowledgements, I would particularly like to thank Derek Barber for so generously making so many of his old photographs of Hadleigh available for publication and for his kind assistance in providing information about the village. Thanks, too, to Bob Delderfield for making much of his own photographic collection available and for sharing his knowledge of Hadleigh people and places.

I would also like to thank Ken Crowe of Southend Museums Service and the staff at the Chelmsford and Southend branches of the Essex Record Office for the large amount of time and effort they spent helping me with my researches.

Apart from the photographic acknowledgements, I would also like to thank the following people and organisations for their help in providing me with information about Hadleigh and, in the case of old Hadleigh residents, for sharing their memories of the village with me: Allied Domecq Inns Ltd; Reverend George Thompson Brake; Jim and John Clubb; Colchester Museum Resource Centre (especially Paul Sealey and Tom Hodgson); Essex County Council (including Dave Buckley, Caroline Ingle, Richard Rigby and Anna White); Susan Gough and colleagues at Southend Library; George Halls; Ian Hook (Essex Regiment Museum); Paul and Lyn Howard; Peter and Mildred Howard; Reverend and Mrs. Ketley; Margaret Masters; Joyce MacConnell; Mr. S. Moss; Alf Permain; Sheila Pitt-Stanley; Hilda Quarterman; Mr. and Mrs. K. Ross; Roy and colleagues at Hadleigh Fire Station; the Salvation Army (especially Beverley Egan, Philip Hendy, Gordon Taylor and Judith Walker); Mr. and Mrs. Tanner; Nick Wickenden (Chelmsford Museums Service). Thanks also to John and Stephen for allowing me access to their homes at Leigh Park Farm and to Fay and Keith at the Mayor's Office in Southend for their help with the John H. Burrows photo. I would particularly like to thank my wife Alison for bearing with me and offering support as Hadleigh took over my life and I would also like to thank Phillimore & Co. Ltd. for bearing me in mind for the project in the first place.

CHAPTER I

Early History

Introduction

From the railway, an expanse of fields dotted with buildings and workshops, and on the top of one of the small hills the grey ruins of two towers looking grimly across the mouth of the Thames. From the turnpike road, a typical English village, quaint and quiet, with a mile-long, curving street of cottages and small shops, an old church, and two or three houses behind smooth lawns and big trees. That is Hadleigh.

Thus did the writer of *Hadleigh—The Story of a Great Endeavour* see the village at the turn of the century, a time of great significance in Hadleigh's history, when it was just on the verge of evolving from a village to a town.

The view from the railway has not significantly changed, but the 'quaint and quiet' village has grown into a bustling urban area, the 'turnpike road' throngs with traffic and the houses with 'smooth lawns and big trees' have now largely been replaced by shops and car showrooms.

Nevertheless, Hadleigh retains much of its ancient character. Its Norman church dominates the village centre, albeit now surrounded by a one-way traffic system and shops, and Hadleigh Castle, the village's most famous landmark, survives as a picturesque ruin two-thirds of a mile to the south.

Some 35 miles from London, Hadleigh grew up on the main road from the Capital which wound its way via Rayleigh to Leigh-on-Sea. It remained, however, a comparatively small settlement of just a few hundred people until 1891, when the Salvation Army arrived to establish a Farm Colony and sparked a population boom that was almost to treble the number of inhabitants there within a decade.

The ancient parish of Hadleigh, now part of the Borough of Castle Point, stretched from the Thames estuary in the south to Pound Wood in the north, with Leigh-on-Sea and South Benfleet parishes to the east and west respectively. Part of Canvey Island, whose rich agricultural land was shared out among several 'mainland' parishes, also belonged to Hadleigh.

Early History

The very earliest origins of the village remain obscure. Some ancient flintwork has been found in neighbouring Daws Heath and Thundersley, to the north and west respectively, and there have been odd finds of Stone-Age implements, but these have not been sufficient to determine the extent of early occupation with any certainty.

The first period when it can fairly definitely be said that there was some sort of early occupation is the Iron Age, and there are two good sites of evidence locally.

The first is in the vicinity of Sayers Farm, to the south west of the village, where some late

1 A late Iron-Age grog-tempered wheel-thrown pot discovered at Sayers Farm in 1936. It may have been used as part of a cremation burial.

2 An aerial photograph of the so-called 'Roman Fort' site in the fields to the south of Hadleigh. Some think that this may actually be an Iron-Age earthwork, since the double enclosure pattern showing up in the crops is similar to that identified at other confirmed Iron-Age sites.

Iron-Age pottery was found in 1936. Some evidence of human cremation burials was also uncovered.

Fifty years later, in 1986, an archaeological dig by Essex County Council on land off Chapel Lane—now the streets called Galleydene and Mountnessing—revealed probably the best evidence of early domestic occupation. Here was discovered a section of what appeared to be a square enclosure, surrounded by a ditch up to a third of a metre deep, which contained two distinct layers of soil and revealed numerous finds. These included 15 pieces of worked flint, a triangular loom weight and over 400 sherds of domestic pottery, mainly from jars and bowls. The site has since been dated either to the Late Bronze or Early Iron Age.

A short distance to the south east is a site of similar interest yet to be excavated. Located by aerial photography in c.1950, this distinctive rectangular earthwork has generally been thought to be a Roman fort or signal station, possibly connected in some

way with the Forts of the Saxon Shore (a chain of forts erected by the Romans to defend the south and east coasts against Saxon invaders). Now, however, there is a school of thought that it could be from the Iron Age, since it bears some similarity with Iron-Age sites elsewhere, including the Chapel Lane one. Excavation is required to prove this either way.

The Chapel Lane and 'Roman fort' sites are both situated on a ridge of ground some 200 feet high which overlooks the River Thames. This would have been an ideal location for human occupation, being close to the river for transport and water, yet high enough above it to escape flooding and to provide a good vantage point for the sighting of enemy ships. The Thames originally came to the foot of the hills which support these sites, but much of the area which was once underwater has now been reclaimed as fertile agricultural land.

The former coastal area between the foot of the hills and where the railway line is now, has revealed

3 Roman bricks at Hadleigh Castle, shaped into a hearth during the 16th century. These and other Roman finds, both at the Castle and elsewhere in the village, provide good evidence of probable Roman occupation in the area.

some good evidence of Roman occupation, particularly in the form of so-called 'Red Hills'. These are thought to be remnants of Roman salt-making operations and can be found at numerous sites around the Essex coast. Most of those in Hadleigh have been ploughed out, but they, and other sites dotted around the lower hills, have revealed a range of Roman finds, including briquetage, pottery sherds and a small bronze figure, possibly a Lar (a figure in the image of a god which symbolised protection over a person or place). Roman items have also been found in various other places in the locality, including odd finds of single coins.

The Saxons followed the Romans into the area and they, too, have left some evidence of their occupation. A site in the centre of Hadleigh, to the immediate south east of the church, was excavated in 1968 and revealed definite evidence of a Saxon child burial and possible additional indications of Iron-Age inhabitation. A rampart and ditch construction was also unearthed there.

The name 'Hadleigh' itself derives from the Saxons' description of the area as a 'haep leah', or 'heath clearing'. The Saxons followed their forefathers in clearing areas of Essex woodland (which was once very extensive) in order to create usable agricultural land. At Hadleigh the area they cleared evolved into Hadleigh village and there is much evidence in the surviving woodland in the north of the parish to show that the Saxons were there.

4 Saxon woodbanks in Poors Lane, dividing Hadleigh Great Wood on the left from Dodd's Grove on the right. These earthen banks were used to mark the boundaries of woodland ownership.

5 Hadleigh church, showing Norman features (exterior).

Much of the woodland that was around in Saxon times has now disappeared, but the ancient names of the individual woods survive and several of these have Saxon derivations. Evidence of Saxon activity can still be seen in so-called 'woodbanks', raised banks of earth used to mark the boundaries of woodland ownership. Several good examples survive, notably on either side of Poors Lane between Hadleigh Great Wood and Dodd's Grove.

The Saxons were succeeded by the Normans, who arrived via the Battle of Hastings in 1066 and recorded in Domesday Book 20 years later the state of the nation they took over. Hadleigh is not mentioned in Domesday Book and it is generally thought that the village is included within the Honor of Rayleigh. (An Honor was a group of estates held as one landholding.)

The Honor of Rayleigh was owned at the time of the Conquest by Robert Fitzwimarc who, unusually for pre-Conquest landowners, kept most of his land after the Normans arrived. By 1086, however, it had passed to his son, Sweyn, who built Rayleigh Castle. On Sweyn's death, the estates passed to his son, Robert, who founded Prittlewell Priory. When Robert died, they passed to his son, Henry de Essex, the King's standard bearer. Unlike his forefathers, however, Henry was destined for disgrace.

According to contemporary sources, Henry was accompanying the King, Henry II, on a campaign in Wales in 1157 when the English were attacked. In the midst of the battle he threw down the standard

and declared that the King had been killed, causing the English to panic and flee. Other noblemen rallied round, however, and it soon became clear that the King was alive and well.

Henry's reputation was tarnished by this event, but he remained in favour for several more years until a personal feud with Robert de Montfort brought memory of his actions to the fore. Robert accused Henry of cowardice in the Welsh campaign and challenged him to a duel. Henry lost and ended his days in a monastery in Reading. All his estates, including the Honor of Rayleigh, were forfeited to the Crown.

It was now up to the King to decide who would inherit Hadleigh next.

Hadleigh Church

One of the great legacies from the Norman period in Hadleigh is the parish church of St James the Less, which occupies the village centre and is very much its focal point. Built *c.*1140 in the reign of

6 Hadleigh church, showing Norman features (interior). The two photographs on this page show interior and exterior views of the Norman apse of Hadleigh church (its semi-circular east end). This is a rare architectural feature to have survived, but is typical of Norman design. The church is one of the great legacies of the Norman period in Hadleigh and remains largely unaltered from its original pattern.

7 A sketch of the 15th-century wallpainting of St George and the dragon discovered under plaster on the south wall of the church during restoration work in 1855 and captured for posterity by J. Parish.

King Stephen, it is older than Hadleigh Castle, something which many visitors find hard to believe.

There may well have been an earlier church on the site and the building's construction, with thick walls and narrow windows, is such as to imply fortification (perhaps in defence against coastal attack) as well as a use for religious purposes. It is built largely of Kentish ragstone, which was probably brought directly across the Thames by boat. A comparatively small church, with a semi-circular east end, or apse, St James' has survived virtually unaltered over the centuries because the village's population remained small until the start of the present century, so there was no need to enlarge it to meet the needs of a growing congregation. Some of the nave windows were altered or added in the 13th to 15th centuries and the porch and weatherboarded belfry are both later additions, but there has been no wholesale enlargement.

Some of the building's most notable features are to be found inside. An array of wall paintings was discovered in the 1850s during restoration work and fragments of two of these survive to this day. The full set of pictures, revealed when plaster was stripped from the inside walls, included Jacobean texts, the Lord's Prayer and the Ten Commandments, a brightly coloured 15th-century representation of St George and the dragon, some angels and a picture of Thomas à Becket. Only the Becket painting and an angel survive—the others did not fare well after being revealed to the air.

8 The painting of Thomas à Becket, which dates from the late 12th century. It is the best surviving example of the paintings which were discovered at Hadleigh Church during the 1855 restoration.

9 The Royal Arms of Queen Anne, dating from after the Union with Scotland (i.e. from *c.*1707 to *c.*1714). They are on display on the north wall of the church.

11 An engraving of the original font at Hadleigh Church. The diagonal stiff-leaf design survives, but the base and bowl have been substantially altered.

The Becket painting, incorporating the words 'Beatus Tomas' (Blessed Thomas), is probably the more impressive of the two and can be clearly seen on the splay of the most easterly window on the north side of the nave. It is thought by most sources to date from *c.*1170-73.

The angel picture, which is in another north wall window splay, probably dates from the 13th century.

Other items of note inside the church include the Royal Arms of Queen Anne (dating from after the Union with Scotland) and some 19th-century stained glass windows, dedicated to various members of the Wood family, major local landowners in the mid- to late 19th century. The font, a composite piece, still exhibits evidence of its Norman origins.

St James has only one bell: a secondhand one dating from 1636 which was bought to replace two others which had been stolen. The communion cup and registers for Hadleigh date back to 1568, while the rectors can be traced to 1216.

Historically, the right of appointment of the rector at Hadleigh belonged to the Crown, though later patrons included the Earls of Warwick (and their descendants), Lincoln College and various private individuals. The Church also owned a small herd of cows and sheep, which it rented out to landowners in return for a fee towards caring for the poor and lighting sacred images in the church.

10 The original Elizabethan Communion Cup from Hadleigh Church, dating from 1568. The full inscription, visible around the lip, reads 'HADLE OF ESSEX BY THE CASTIEL'.

12 The rectors' board in Hadleigh Church, listing the rectors from 1216.

The church's surroundings have regrettably deteriorated over the years as Hadleigh has evolved from a rural community into an urban one and it is now surrounded by a one-way system and a bustling shopping area. Nevertheless, the 'unsightly shops and shacks near its east end' which the eminent architectural historian, Sir Nikolaus Pevsner, encountered there in the 1950s have long since been demolished and the churchyard itself remains surprisingly peaceful. Its position on the main road also makes it one of the best known landmarks in the area—something it has been for over 800 years.

CHAPTER II

Hadleigh Castle and its Ownership

The Royal Park

Following the disgrace of Henry de Essex, the lands at Hadleigh reverted to the Crown. These, together with lands at Rayleigh, Thundersley and Eastwood were now used by the King as Royal Parks for hunting. The park at Hadleigh was roughly in the vicinity of Park Farm—on the open fields to the east of the village, south of the London Road—and its outline can still be traced in field boundaries on maps of Hadleigh from the late 19th century.

Deer were the main quarry in the parks and records show that animals were often sent to the King's table in London. Fish from park fishponds also ended up there. The parklands had additional value in their timber, which was sold to raise money or used in shipbuilding or general construction. Timber from the parks and the woodland to the north of Hadleigh was used at both the Tower of London and Westminster Abbey. It may also have found a use locally, at Prittlewell Priory and Southchurch Hall.

The parks were not popular with villagers, who were banned from using the vast resources they offered and so lost a valuable source of their own food and fuel, as well as of food for their animals.

In 1231 the history of Hadleigh reached one of its first important milestones, when a licence was issued to authorise construction of the village's most famous building—Hadleigh Castle.

Hadleigh Castle Origins

Hadleigh's church may be older, but its castle has for centuries attracted more attention. It dates from the time of the next major figure in the locality—Hubert de Burgh.

The major defensive stronghold in the Honor of Rayleigh was Sweyn's castle at Rayleigh, which stood on the site known as Rayleigh Mount. Along with Hadleigh manor, this was forfeited to the Crown

by the actions of Henry de Essex in the latter half of the 12th century.

By the turn of the 13th century, however, King John was on the throne and facing uprisings from various Norman barons and baron-inspired invasions from France. Throughout John's troubled reign—and that of his son, Henry III—Hubert de Burgh was to be one of the Crown's greatest allies.

Hubert De Burgh

De Burgh was born in Norfolk in c.1175 and probably saw service as a boy to John's immediate predecessor and brother, Richard I. He was John's chamberlain by 1198 and in June 1215, just after Magna Carta, was made justiciar, the chief judicial officer of the realm. He supported the King both politically and on the battlefield. His military exploits included a superb defence of Dover Castle against the French King's son, Prince Louis (with English baronial backing), in 1216 and a second successful defence the following year. He also defeated a French invasionary force of 80 ships in 1217 in England's first large-scale naval victory, the Battle of Sandwich.

The death of King John in 1216 brought about a compromise peace between the Crown and the barons, and John's successor, Henry III, was looked after by the regent, William Marshall. When Marshall died in 1219, De Burgh became the dominant figure in government.

Amongst the innumerable possessions given to him by John and Henry in reward for his service were the Manor of Rayleigh and the Manor of Hadleigh. He quickly set about building a castle at the latter, where the Thameside location offered a better chance of repelling any French invasions than did Sweyne's old castle at Rayleigh.

De Burgh's dominance in government and favouritism with the King made him several enemies.

13　Hadleigh Castle from the air, viewed from the east and showing in the foreground the two main surviving towers. Entry to the castle was originally gained from this direction but the entrance was later moved to the north-west corner (top right in the picture) to improve security. Note also the effect of landslides on the left-hand side which has led to the south wall falling down the hill.

The barons were agitating for concessions and several failed military expeditions in Wales and the continuing loss of English-held lands in France contributed to the growing unrest. As the young King reached maturity he began to hanker after reclaiming lands in France that had been lost by his father, and the barons began to poison his mind with ideas about the alleged treachery of Hubert De Burgh.

In 1232, on largely trumped-up charges, De Burgh was arrested and dismissed from office. He spent two years detained in Merton Priory and Devizes Castle during several trials and retrials and at one stage was dragged (against the traditional rules of refuge) from the sanctuary at Brentwood chapel and taken to the Tower of London. After a period of imprisonment, he was eventually released and pardoned. He was reconciled with the King to a degree, but never regained the power or authority that he had once wielded. He died in 1243 at

Banstead in Surrey. His castle at Hadleigh reverted to the Crown, but his wife, Margaret, retained possession of Hadleigh manor.

Hubert De Burgh's Castle

Hubert De Burgh's lasting legacy to Hadleigh was his castle. In design it was not a typical Norman motte-and-bailey construction. It probably took the form of an octagonal bailey, with a buttressed curtain wall and small angle towers. Its entrance was probably to the east where a natural long shallow hill feature, known locally as the Saddleback, leads down to the marshland below. This would have given good access to the sea, which came up to the foot of the hill in those days, and it may also have doubled as a training ground for castle knights. Inside the bailey there was a hall with a solar (a living or withdrawing room connected to the hall) and several other buildings. The castle walls were nine feet

14 The only known picture of Hubert de Burgh, builder of Hadleigh Castle, taken from a 14th-century manuscript and showing him seeking sanctuary in the chapel at Brentwood following his fall from grace in 1232.

thick at the base and the area enclosed was just over an acre.

The building occupied a good site, with a vantage point over the river, access to the main road at Hadleigh village and steep, largely natural, defensive prospects on all sides. Much of the stone used in its construction was brought by water across the Thames from Kent. Evidence of this was obtained during the construction of the London-Tilbury-Southend railway in the mid-19th century, when navvies discovered the remains of some sunken barges, laden with Kentish ragstone, 12 feet below ground.

After De Burgh

After De Burgh's death and the reversion of the castle to the Crown, the building fell into comparative disuse. The Sheriff of Essex had already surveyed it for the King in 1240 and discovered it needed repair. Further repairs were required in 1256 after the King's agent, Stephen de Salines, had let it become ruinous, with walls and roofs both requiring attention.

In the early 14th century, with Edward II now on the throne, some more work was carried out, with the construction of a chamber above the main gate and a chamber and a new gate at the postern (a small entrance at the back of the building). Some alterations were made to the barbican (an outwork which defended the castle entrance) and repairs were carried out to the curtain wall. Several minor repairs were also effected in the cellar, hall, kitchen and larder.

Hadleigh itself was still little more than a few houses clustered around the church and a large area of parkland, but it did have sheep breeding on the marshes and a large common to the north west of the church. It also had a market, which had been granted by charter as early as 1246.

The parish also possessed a watermill at the foot of the Saddleback ridge to the east of the castle, though the products of this were probably seen by the castle's occupants rather than by the villagers. The mill lasted until at least 1627 and its site was still visible in the 19th century.

Some Early Owners and Occupants

During the 13th century the castle went through several changes of ownership, often reverting to the Crown in between. It was also often in the guardianship of a constable, appointed to look after it on behalf of the King.

In 1268 it was in the possession of Richard De Tany or (Thany), but by 1299 it was owned by Edward I's second wife, Margaret, having been given to her (along with Hadleigh town and park) as part of her dowry. By 1312 it was in the custody of Roger Filiol on her behalf.

Edward III Rebuild

By the time of Edward III's accession, there was trouble again with France. The Hundred Years War was about to begin and Edward was looking to strengthen his defences.

He did this at Hadleigh by a large-scale re-building of the castle c.1360-70. The curtain wall was strengthened and new towers erected. The steep sides and ditches around it were enhanced and the

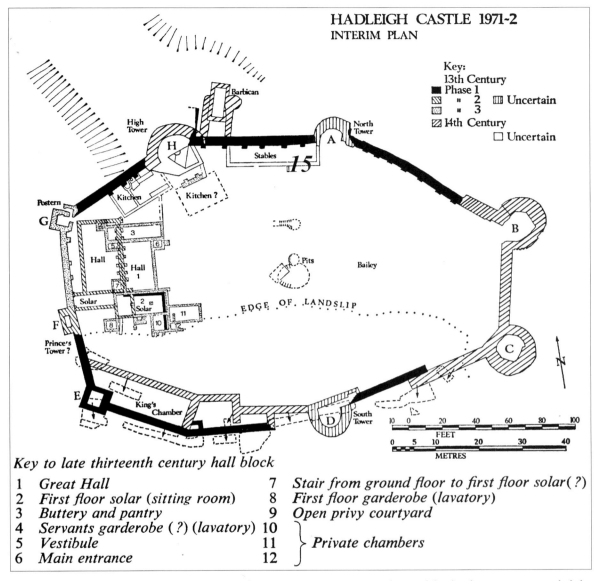

HADLEIGH CASTLE 1971-2
INTERIM PLAN

Key:
13th Century
■ Phase 1
▨ " 2   ▥ Uncertain
▦ " 3
▨ 14th Century
□ Uncertain

Barbican

High Tower

North Tower

H   A

Stables

15

Kitchen   Kitchen ?

Postern

G   B

3

5   6

Hall   Hall
            1

Solar   Pits   Bailey

2
Solar

8   10   11

EDGE OF LANDSLIP

F

Prince's
Tower ?

C

N

E   D   South
      King's   Tower
      Chamber

10 0   20   40   60   80   100
            FEET
0   5 10   20   30   40
            METRES

Key to late thirteenth century hall block

1	*Great Hall*
2	*First floor solar (sitting room)*
3	*Buttery and pantry*
4	*Servants garderobe (?) (lavatory)*
5	*Vestibule*
6	*Main entrance*

7	*Stair from ground floor to first floor solar (?)*
8	*First floor garderobe (lavatory)*
9	*Open privy courtyard*
10	
11	*Private chambers*
12	

15 A ground plan of Hadleigh Castle showing the various stages in the castle's development as revealed by archaeological excavation.

entrance was moved from the east to the north west, an easier position to defend and one which gave better access to the main road. More ragstone was introduced and a strong mortar of lime, sand and seashells, many brought from nearby Canvey Island, was used to bind the construction together. A new 'high tower' and barbican were built at the north-west corner to defend the new entrance. Inside the walls, improvements were also carried out to the residential quarters to make them fit for Royal occupation. A new great hall was built, plus a new

kitchen and some stables. Money to finance some of this rebuilding was almost certainly raised from the sale of timber and animals in the Royal Parks.

Despite its strengthening, the castle never saw any serious action and its ruinous condition today owes more to wanton vandalism in the 16th century and to later landslides than it does to warfare. The ruins which are visible today date partly from the original castle of Hubert De Burgh and partly from the Edward III rebuilding, with a few minor additions in between. The south-east and north-east towers are the most complete survivors, though much of the original curtain wall also remains. The foundations of some of the interior buildings can also be seen in the grass. Even in its ruined state, however, it is still probably the most important later medieval castle in Essex.

Later Owners and Occupants

After Edward III's interest and the wars with France were over, the castle once again went through a succession of owners.

Aubrey De Vere was owner at the time of his death in 1400 and shortly after that the building was in the ownership of Edmund, Duke of York. It was also later in the ownership of Edward, Earl of Rutland, and Humphrey, Duke of Gloucester.

A previous Duke of Gloucester, Thomas, had visited the castle in death when his body was brought back from Calais, where he had been murdered on the orders of Richard II, and the ship carrying it anchored beneath the castle before onward transition for burial in Pleshey.

By the 1450s the castle had been given to Edmund, Earl of Richmond, brother of Henry VI.

16 Richard, Lord Rich, who was probably responsible for the systematic demolition of Hadleigh Castle in the mid-16th century. By this stage, the castle had outlived its usefulness and its valuable stonework was taken for building projects elsewhere. Rich, a shrewd and successful politician, had seats at Leez Priory and Rochford, as well as his lands at Hadleigh.

The grant for this also included the manor of Hadleigh, the advowson of the church, various local mills and permission to administer the local fisheries and operate a weekly Wednesday market, presumably the one begun in 1246. Later still, it was in the possession of Elizabeth Woodville, wife (and Queen) of Edward IV.

When Henry VIII was king the castle and manor were successively granted to three of the much-married monarch's wives: Catherine of Aragon *c*.1510, Anne of Cleves *c*.1540 and Catherine Parr *c*.1543.

By 1552 Edward VI had sold the castle, manor, park and advowson of the church to Richard, Lord Rich, for £700. Rich, a major Essex landowner, had seats at Leez Priory (near Great Leighs) and Rochford. He acquired additional land in Hadleigh shortly afterwards and it was probably he who began a systematic demolition of the castle to re-use its stone elsewhere.

From Rich the castle and much of the land in Hadleigh village descended to the Earls of Warwick, then, through one of six co-heirs, to Henry St John (later Viscount St John). It then passed through several generations to Brigadier General Sir Robert Bernard Sparrow, whose wife, Lady Olivia Sparrow, was to become an important benefactor to the growing Hadleigh village. She died in 1863 and the castle and farmlands were sold to Major Thomas Jenner Spitty of Billericay.

Due to its royal and castle associations, Hadleigh was alternatively known throughout much of this period as 'Kyngeshadlegh' and 'Hadley ad Castrum'.

Archaeological Excavations

Much of the early evidence for the history of Hadleigh Castle came from an extensive study by the 19th-century antiquarian, Henry William ('H.W.') King.

Born in 1816, King was the eldest son of William Henry King, a customs officer at Leigh-on-Sea, and was a leading member of the Essex Archaeological Society, writing many articles in society publications. He married Jane Wood, a member of a distinguished Hadleigh family, in 1837 and, with his son, Montague, carried out a series of excavations at the castle throughout the spring and summer of 1863.

King was well aware of the importance of his excavations in the on-going story of Hadleigh Castle. It was the first serious attempt to study accurately the history of the building and to reproduce it diagrammatically in an accurate way. Previous pictures had been somewhat fanciful in their interpretation of the building. Even John Constable's

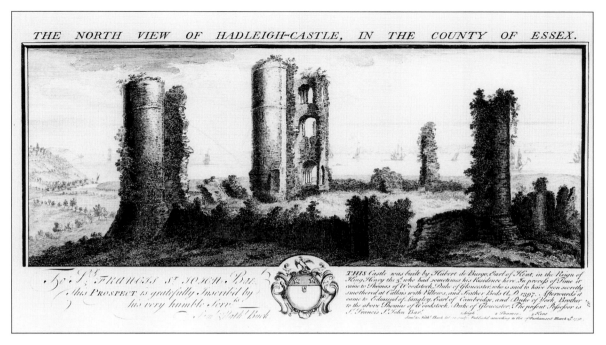

THE NORTH VIEW OF HADLEIGH-CASTLE, IN THE COUNTY OF ESSEX.

17 & 18 Many of the early pictorial representations of Hadleigh Castle took on a somewhat fanciful appearance. The 18th century in particular seems to have had a wealth of drawings of this kind available. Later artists tended largely to try to recreate the castle's original appearance, based on modern archaeological evidence.

19   Hadleigh Castle

20   A sketch of Hadleigh Castle made by H.W. King in 1850, 13 years before his principal excavations took place. King was well aware that no serious attempt had hitherto been made to document the history of the castle and made every effort to do so accurately himself. This is therefore probably one of the most reliable representations of how the castle actually looked in the mid-19th century.

famous and powerful castle picture, displayed full-scale at the Royal Academy in 1829 after a visit to Hadleigh in 1814, contains a touch of artistic licence.

The plans and sketches which accompanied King's report, often drawn by more competent artists than himself, were reproduced in various editions of the Essex Archaeological Society's *Transactions* during the 1860s.

Areas investigated by King included the south tower, the bailey, the north-west tower beside the new Edward III entrance, the original kitchen and the postern. Amongst other things, his work revealed the presence of buildings within the bailey and identified the most likely water-source for castle occupants as being via a pipe from nearby Plumtree Hill. He also found animal bones, glass, pottery and tiles within the bailey area, though overall he located very few important specific finds. King's colleague, John Sparvel-Bayley, did a lot of research into historical documents, which supported King's archaeological work. King also reported on the discovery, just prior to his castle excavations,

21 The grave of H.W. King in Hadleigh churchyard. King did much to uncover the history of Hadleigh Castle and was married to a member of the Wood family, major Hadleigh landowners in the mid- to late 19th century.

22 Excavations in progress at Hadleigh Castle during the early 1970s. These were the most detailed excavations to be made at the castle and revealed several important clues to the history of the building, as well as a number of interesting finds.

23 Excavations in progress at Hadleigh Castle in the early 1970s.

24 A selection of pottery items found at Hadleigh Castle during the 1971–2 excavations. Most of them date from the medieval period.

of the site of the park-keeper's lodge from the old Royal Park.

H.W. King died in 1893 and is buried in Hadleigh churchyard.

★   ★   ★

The next major excavations after King were not carried out until 1971-2, when P.L. Drewett made an even more thorough investigation of the site. These excavations took place just after a landslip in the winter of 1969-70 which carried some of the southern curtain wall and internal building foundations down the cliff. This was by no means the first landslip at the site and it was largely the inevitable result of constructing heavy stonework on a comparatively unstable geological base.

The excavations in 1971 included a great deal of work at the western end of the bailey, where the 1969-70 landslip had revealed some previously unknown foundations. They confirmed the existence of a small hall and solar, built over the top of an earlier hall and solar which had evidently collapsed sometime in the period between Hubert de Burgh's works and Edward III's. They also revealed a 16th-century hearth which had been used to melt down lead from the castle when the materials from it were being taken away by Lord Rich's men.

An exploratory trench was dug across the bailey, at right angles to the northern curtain wall, and this revealed a medieval chalk-lined pit (possibly for the storage of live shellfish), the foundations of some stables and various bits of flooring. Further work was carried out at the north-west tower, revealing it to have been built on top of earlier stonework and also leading to the discovery of a socket for a portcullis.

In 1972 additional research revealed yet more bailey buildings, including private chambers, a buttery and pantry and the new (Edward III) kitchen. Traces were also found of a possible, even earlier, hall than the two discovered in 1971.

The western tower, known as the 'garderobe tower', was also investigated and this revealed a substantial amount of pottery and hundreds of fish, bird and animal bones. Excavations were also made at the barbican, where the pivot of a wooden bridge over a pit was discovered. The pit was probably filled in by Lord Rich's men, since it contained largely rubbish items of little or no value.

By the time of their completion, the excavations had revealed a whole range of items from various periods, including pottery, building material, window glass, floor tiles, coins, pre-castle (i.e. Roman, etc.) material, various items of metalwork (knives, keys, buckles, etc.) and an array of bird, fish and mammal bones.

Today

Hadleigh Castle is today open to the public, free of charge. The site is run by English Heritage and is a popular recreational amenity.

CHAPTER III

The Early Development of Hadleigh Village

Despite all this activity at the castle, Hadleigh village remained remarkably quiet. It consisted for centuries of little more than a few houses clustered around the church and an area of common land to the north-west on which the villagers could feed and exercise their animals. Much of the land to the south-east remained out-of-bounds while the Royal Park was in existence, whilst dense woodland occupied the northernmost part of the parish. Largely rural and agricultural, Hadleigh remained a quiet, uninterrupted backwater for around 500 years.

The Park and Fisheries

As the castle declined in importance and much of the land in the old Hadleigh manor found its way into private ownership, it could not be long before the Royal Park also fell into disuse. It is last mentioned in the records in the 16th century, though its outline could still be traced in field boundaries almost until the start of the present century.

In Benfleet Creek and Hadleigh Ray, the waters below the castle which separated the parish from Canvey Island, there was a long tradition of fishing which, though not as important to Hadleigh as to neighbouring Leigh-on-Sea, was nonetheless a valuable amenity to those entitled to fish there.

The fishery at Hadleigh was a much prized possession, often leading to disputes in ownership, court cases and even physical violence. In 1724 a 'Kentish Armada' sailed across the Thames and removed 1,000 bushels of oysters from Hadleigh Ray. The fishery was still important enough to its owner 140 years later to warrant a court case against a neighbour who was intending to stop up part of the waterway to the detriment of the plaintiff's oyster and mussel stocks.

With keen competition for catches of fish in the neighbourhood there were many disputes between the fishery owners and fishermen from Leigh. Cases are recorded as far back as Lord Rich's time and crop up periodically about once every 50 or 60 years until at least the late 1880s.

The village got one side benefit from Leigh's thriving fishing industry—the Leigh shrimp carts, which travelled through Hadleigh on their way to the London markets, offered a convenient, if uncomfortable, ride to the Capital.

The Market and Fair

Hadleigh's market, which had been established by charter in 1246, was still in operation as late as the 15th century but it is not known exactly when it died out. The village also had its own fair at one stage and this was still going in the latter part of the 19th century. White's *Directory of Essex* (1848) records that it was a fair for 'pleasure and pedlery', held annually on 24 June.

One of the best descriptions of the fair is provided by the novelist, Arthur Morrison, whose book *Cunning Murrell* gives a colourful account of life in the village in the mid- to late 19th century. Some allowance must be made for it being fictional, but much of the rest of the novel is based on fact, so there is no reason to suspect that his description of the fair is any different.

According to Morrison 'it was the way of the Hadleigh Fair to begin betimes on Midsummer's Day morning, so that it had pushed Hadleigh village almost out of sight before breakfast'. Attractions included the Fat Lady, the Living Skeleton and 'on one fair in three, the Fire-eater of Madagascar, when free from engagements before all the Crowned Heads'. There had, wrote Morrison, 'been two Mermaids within living recollection, though the last, as a sight, was considered unworthy the penny admission; but the really great exhibitions that graced Rayleigh Fair a month earlier—Wombwell's, Clarke's, Johnson and Lee's—rarely or ever took a stand at Hadleigh'.

25 Chapman and André's 1777 map of the Hadleigh area, one of the best early visual representations of the village.

26 A plaque commemorating the site of the ancient Burnt Oak on the main road to the east of Hadleigh. The oak marked the boundary of the village with the manor of Southchurch. The modern-day boundary between Hadleigh (in the borough of Castle Point) and Leigh-on-Sea (in Southend) still runs through this point.

Stalls selling bull's eyes, peppermints, spice nuts, gingernuts, songsheets, toys, textiles, ribbons, garters, china and watches mingled with booths, peepshows, wigwams and stands of all kinds to transform the village into a temporary town. Visitors came from neighbouring parishes to feast on gooseberry pie— 'the crown, glory, high symbol, and fetish of Hadleigh Fair'. The pubs were filled with merry-makers from dawn 'til dusk and a 'customary fight' took place between the natives of Hadleigh and fishermen from Leigh-on-Sea.

Chapman and André

One of the best early visual representations of Hadleigh is provided by the celebrated map of Essex by John Chapman and Peter André which was published in 1777. One of the first really accurate large-scale maps to be produced, it shows, as expected, the 'Ruins of Hadley Castle' and 'Hadley Park' (the old Royal Parkland which had by now become Park Farm). It also shows another important

farm in Hadleigh's history, Castle Farm (named on the map as 'Hadley Lordships').

Very little detail of the village itself is recorded, but 'Hadley Common' and the cluster of houses around the church can both be clearly seen. Rectory Road leads north from the church towards Daws Heath and the embryonic Scrub and Poors Lanes can also be made out. An area of woodland sweeps in an almost unbroken arc around the north of the village, though there are several inaccuracies in the naming of individual woods.

On the main road to the east of the village 'The Burnt Oak' marks the eastern boundary of the parish. This name is centuries old and a commemorative plaque identifying the site of the original oak can still be seen there today.

The Road Through Hadleigh

As time went on, the main road through the village gradually developed from a badly maintained dirt track, used by people and, occasionally, horses, into a more substantial road that could carry wheeled vehicles.

In the early days of highway maintenance the repair of each stretch of road was the responsibility of the landowner whose property it bordered. Not all landowners took this responsibility seriously and journeys could often be rough and uncomfortable. The Highways Act of 1555 sought to resolve this problem by removing the responsibility for the upkeep of roads from such landowners and introducing instead the concept of all local people being responsible for the upkeep of local roads. In practice this meant that each parish had to elect two highway surveyors to monitor the condition of local roads and every family had either to pay for labourers to carry out any necessary repairs or to do the work themselves. As wheeled vehicles became increasingly common this became quite a burdensome task and those who chose not to fulfil their obligations were regularly brought before the authorities.

To resolve some of the impracticalities of this form of road-mending, the concept of toll-roads or turnpikes was introduced, whereby those using the road would be the ones who actually paid for its upkeep. This was a much better arrangement where the main roads were concerned because villagers living on routes used by hundreds of non-locals would otherwise find themselves paying ridiculously large sums for the upkeep of roads to the benefit of others.

Though Hadleigh itself was small, the road through it from London to Leigh was sufficiently used to warrant the establishment of a turnpike, which was set up by an Act of Parliament in 1747

27 The turnpike cottage stood at the north-east corner of what is now Victoria House Corner, when that junction was still a staggered crossroads. It was demolished before the Second World War and would probably by now have been in the centre of the Victoria House Corner roundabout. The house on the left (at the top of Rayleigh Road) is still there.

as part of a scheme authorising the Essex Turnpike Trust to implement turnpike arrangements on the road from Shenfield to Leigh, through Rayleigh and Hadleigh. The 18th century was the golden age of turnpike construction and by 1793 traffic had evidently increased so much that a second turnpike road was brought into operation between Hadleigh and Bread and Cheese Hill in Thundersley to the west of the village. The tollhouse for the original turnpike from Rayleigh was situated at the *Woodman's Arms* crossroads in Thundersley, whilst that for the second turnpike from Bread and Cheese Hill stood at what is now the roundabout road junction, Victoria House Corner.

From 1793 to 1820 the road through Bread and Cheese Hill was run by the Hadleigh Turnpike Trust, apparently with limited success. In the years 1817-20 the Hadleigh turnpike was collecting an average of £220 per year in tolls. By 1861, however, Hadleigh parishioners were voting for the complete abolition of turnpikes.

The Railway

By the mid-19th century the once-popular turnpikes had been superseded by the railways and new lines sprang up between major towns all over the country. Such was the comparative unimportance of Hadleigh at this time that when the railway came to south-east Essex it passed the village by. No doubt the location of the village centre, high on the hill above the reclaimed marshland across which the railway was to run from South Benfleet to Leigh-on-Sea, had something to do with the lack of provision of a station, but the population of the village had hardly changed for centuries and the settlement was evidently not considered important enough to warrant a costly diversion of the line.

In the 1880s a more direct line from London to South Benfleet, across the marshes between Upminster and Pitsea (instead of via Tilbury), drastically shortened the journey time between the area and the Capital, but still no station was provided. The new line brought more traffic and some

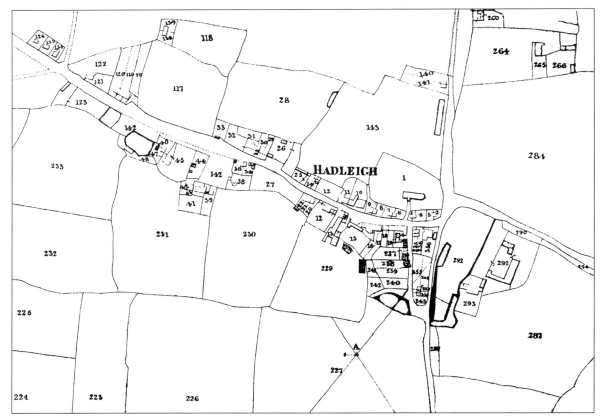

28   The Tithe Map for Hadleigh of 1847. Parcels of land were numbered to identify who owned them and from this information an idea of the extent of the landholdings of individuals in the village can easily be obtained. The map shows the situation 70 years on from Chapman and André, but there has been very little development and most of the houses are still clustered around the High Street and Endway to the south of the church (number 1 on the map). Note the cottages in front of the church, which have long-since disappeared.

expansion to neighbouring South Benfleet, but Hadleigh remained sufficiently remote to be unaffected.

The Tithe Map

The Tithe Map for Hadleigh of 1847 gives full details of the village's landowners and occupants at this time and provides a good general picture of the layout of the village in the mid-19th century. The common still stretched extensively around the north-western fringe of the village and the old Royal Park boundary to the south-east was now separating the landholdings of Park Farm from those of Hadleigh Hall in the High Street.

Hadleigh itself was still little more than a row of houses and shops stretching approximately from the junction with Rectory Road and Castle Lane at the eastern end to Chapel Lane (then called Workhouse Lane) at the western end. There were one or two buildings further west, such as Hadleigh House,

which stood to the south west of Victoria House Corner, and the only other buildings were odd farms dotted around the village centre.

Hadleigh Hall

The most easterly building in the main street of the village at this time was Hadleigh Hall, which stood, set back, on the south-east side of the junction between the High Street and Castle Lane. It was originally in the possession of the Heber family, but at the time of the Tithe Award was in the ownership of Jonathan Wood junior.

The Hebers were an ancient Hadleigh family, but their last known member, Reginald, died in 1793 without issue. Blind for the last part of his life, he was buried in a vault on the south side of the church, which his principal heir, John Gowing, had inscribed with the words 'The family is now extinct'. Heber had been baptised in the church in 1709 and was churchwarden for many years. His

29 Hadleigh Hall was one of the most prestigious houses in the village. It was occupied by several important local families, including the Hebers and the Woods. The Woods rebuilt the original hall in the mid-19th century and this picture shows the result. The building was later used by the Salvation Army and it also became the home of a well-known local doctor. It stood to the east of Castle Lane (where the parade of shops is now) and was demolished in 1961.

parents were both buried at Hadleigh and several other members of the family are mentioned in the registers. He left a substantial sum of money in his will to a range of beneficiaries, including his housekeeper and her husband. The *Crown* inn in Hadleigh High Street was one of his properties—left to his servant, Ann Webb.

In the early 1820s the Hall was described as a 'capital mansion', set in 16 acres of pasture land, with 'seven good bedrooms', a dining room, drawing room, parlour, breakfast parlour, vestibule, kitchen, larder, scullery, water closet, washroom, beer and wine cellars and sleeping accommodation for up to 10 servants. The dining parlour and drawing room both had elegant marble chimneys. Outside there was stabling for at least six horses and a coachhouse 'for a four-wheeled carriage and gig'. The Hall had its own walled garden and well, there were lodges at the entrance to the drive and it was fronted by 'a handsome portico, with a flight

of stone steps in front'. Its location on the turnpike road to London and proximity to the 'much frequented bathing place' of Southend made it highly desirable. 'The whole property,' it was said, 'forms a complete residence for a genteel family.'

By the 1830s the property had found its way into the ownership of Lady Charlotte Denys, whose Trustees sold it to the Wood family. It was described in 1837 as being 'adapted for the accommodation of a family of the highest respectability' and its new owners certainly fitted that description.

The Woods were a major landowning family in south-east Essex, with properties in South Benfleet, Leigh, Prittlewell and Canvey Island. The founder of the Hadleigh branch of the family, Henry Wood, appears to have lived in Hadleigh Hall as lessee for some years prior to its purchase. His son Jonathan and grandson Jonathan junior were both prominent members of the community, occupying several important positions in the parish vestry—

30 The grave of Reginald Heber, on the south side of Hadleigh churchyard. Heber lived in Hadleigh Hall and was the last known member of the family when he died in 1793. He left a substantial sum of money and a large amount of property to his many beneficiaries.

31 The only known picture of Jonathan Wood, taken from a photograph of a now-lost painting.

the forerunner of the parish council—including overseer, surveyor and assessor. Jonathan senior was also a long-serving churchwarden.

There are memorial windows to Jonathan and his wife Ann in Hadleigh church and H.W. King, who married Jonathan junior's sister, Jane, is similarly commemorated.

At the time of the 1851 census Jonathan senior, Jonathan junior and Henry junior owned between them almost 2,000 acres. The family, its trustees and its descendants continued to own large tracts of land in the parish for several decades. As late as 1890, Lionel Wood was still one of Hadleigh's principal landowners.

Unfortunately for Hadleigh Hall, however, the Woods' interest in the Hebers' ancient mansion gradually began to wane and, in the 1840s, they demolished it and replaced it with a newer building closer to the road. This building lasted until 1961.

Blossoms

To the west of Hadleigh Hall, a little further down the High Street, was a farmhouse called Blossoms, which stood in the vicinity of what is now Homestead Road. It was originally owned by another ancient Hadleigh family—the Strangmans—who are recorded as being involved with the village as early as the reign of Edward III.

At the time of the Tithe Map, Blossoms was occupied by John Pocklington, though it was in the ownership of Eleazer Tyrrell, one of two farming brothers with land in the parish. The other brother, James, himself lived in Blossoms later on, but Eleazer appears to have remained in his native Horndon-on-the-Hill. According to the 19th-century Rochford Hundred historian, Philip Benton, there was an ancient Hadleigh family called Blossome and the name may well have derived from them.

The Tyrrells were related to the Wood family and, like the Woods, held several important positions

32 Hadleigh High Street showing Blossoms (the double-roofed building on the right), which was one of Hadleigh's ancient farmhouses. It had its own dairy, a walled garden and numerous stables and outbuildings. It stood where the entrance to Homestead Road is now and was demolished during the 1920s. This photograph shows it before the First World War. The houses on the right are now business premises.

on the parish vestry: James Tyrrell was variously overseer, assessor, surveyor and churchwarden.

In 1886, when Blossoms came up for auction, it was 'a desirable family residence … with walled-in gardens, stables, chaise houses, farmyard and buildings and six acres of orchard opposite'. A 'substantially brick-built and tiled' residence, it was enclosed in front by an iron pallisade fence on a dwarf wall and approached by stone steps. There were several bedrooms, a drawing room, entrance hall, dining room, store room, kitchen, scullery, dairy and cellars. Part of the tenure was leasehold, at a peppercorn rent dating from 1651. It was demolished in the 1920s.

Park Farm

To the south of the village, on the hills overlooking the river, there were three more farms. The most easterly was Park Farm, which occupied roughly the site of the old Royal Park. The distinctive open

field on the modern-day London Road to the east of Hadleigh is part of this farm.

At the time of the Tithe Award the farm was owned by the Lady of the Manor, Lady Olivia Sparrow, but was occupied by Henry Wood junior. Lady Sparrow rebuilt the original farmhouse in 1861.

Castle Farm

The second major farm on the Downs beneath the village was Castle Farm. This farm (now known as Home Farm and in the ownership of the Salvation Army) had a long and interesting history, possibly dating back to the 13th or 14th century and being the location of the old manorial court, the only one in Hadleigh parish. The farmhouse was rebuilt in the early years of the 18th century, though this building has itself since been replaced.

The farm was once in the ownership of the Hislip and Masterman families. John Hislip died in 1786 and was buried in Hadleigh churchyard. His

ESSEX,
HADLEIGH & CANVEY ISLAND.

The Particulars and Conditions of Sale

OF

VALUABLE ESTATES,

Situate in the VILLAGE of HADLEIGH, about two miles from the Benfleet and Leigh Stations on the London Tilbury and Southend Railway, seven miles from the Market Town of Rochford, fourteen from the County Town of Chelmsford, and five from the rapidly increasing seaside resort of Southend, comprising a

DESIRABLE FAMILY RESIDENCE

KNOWN AS

"BLOSSOMS,"

With walled-in GARDENS, STABLES, CHAISE HOUSES, FARM YARD and BUILDINGS, and 6a. 0r. 0p. of ACCOMMODATION PASTURE LAND.

SIXTEEN COTTAGES WITH GARDENS,

In the occupation of Messrs. BALLS, PASSFIELD, TOOKEY, SMITH, AUSTIN, RIGWELL, and others; the

BUSINESS PREMISES

With DOUBLE-FRONTED SHOP, DWELLING HOUSE, BAKE OFFICE and APPURTENANCES;

A CAPITAL BRICK-BUILT HOUSE

KNOWN AS

"HAROLD HOUSE,"

With LARGE GARDEN, ORCHARD, STABLE and CHAISE HOUSE;

BRICK AND TIMBER BUILT MESSUAGE

With FARM BUILDINGS, GARDEN, and about Four Acres of PASTURE LAND; also a

VALUABLE FREEHOLD FARM

KNOWN AS

"THE TREE FARM,"

Situate on CANVEY ISLAND, about two miles from the Benfleet Railway Station, comprising

FARM HOUSE, AGRICULTURAL BUILDINGS,

AND

133a. 1r. 3p. of Productive Arable and Pasture Land;

Which will be Sold by Auction, by

MR. T. W. OFFIN,

IN CONJUNCTION WITH

Mr. A. W. TYRRELL,

By Direction of Messrs. Tyrrell,

On Saturday, the 27th day of November, 1886,

AT THE "ROYAL HOTEL," SOUTHEND, ESSEX,

AT THREE O'CLOCK PRECISELY IN THE AFTERNOON.   IN TWELVE LOTS.

The Property may be Viewed upon application to the Auctioneers; and Particulars with Plans and Conditions of Sale obtained of Messrs. WOODARD, HOOD & WELLS, Solicitors, 6, Billiter Street, London, E.C., and Billericay, Essex; at the Place of Sale; of Mr. A. W. TYRRELL, Auctioneer & Surveyor, Wote Street, Basingstoke, Hants; and of Mr T. W. OFFIN, Auctioneer & Estate Agent,

ROCHFORD & RAYLEIGH, ESSEX.

H. KEMSHEAD's Steam Printing Works, Lower Kennington Lane, S.E.

33   A notice advertising the forthcoming auction of the 'desirable family residence known as Blossoms' (and several other properties) in November 1886.

widow married one of the Mastermans, whose family are also buried in the churchyard. According to Benton the last member of the Hadleigh branch of the Masterman family hanged himself in a barn in 1813.

At the time of the Tithe Award Castle Farm was occupied by Jonathan Wood senior on lease from Lady Olivia Sparrow.

Sayers Farm

The furthest west of the three farms on the Downs was Sayers Farm, the farmhouse of which still survives, just beyond the Chapel Lane entrance to Hadleigh Castle Country Park. An earlier farmhouse was probably owned by William Sayer in 1491.

34 A line drawing of Park Farm dating from 1891. Situated on the site of the old Royal Park, the farm was owned in the mid-19th century by Hadleigh's Lady of the Manor, Lady Olivia Sparrow.

At one period it was in the ownership of the Strangman family, but at the time of the Tithe Award it was owned by James Patten, though apparently leased to Daniel and John Woodard, another pair of farming brothers in the village. Over the next few decades the Woodards built up their landholding in Hadleigh and, like the Woods and Tyrrells, were heavily involved in parish affairs. Daniel Woodard was overseer, surveyor and parish constable, whilst John Woodard was a surveyor. A relative, Edward Woodard, a solicitor from Billericay, was of great help to local landowners in their negotiations with the railway company when the line was first constructed.

35 The pond at Park Farm around the turn of the century.

36 The old farmhouse at Castle Farm, which stood on the hill overlooking the marshlands. Dating from the early 18th century, it was demolished in the 1970s. Castle Farm was anciently the site of the only manorial court in Hadleigh and was also at one time occupied by the prosperous Wood family.

37 Sayers Farm, named for its connections with one-time owner, William Sayer, who is thought to have lived there in the late 15th century. The furthest west of the three farms on the Downs, it was also once separately owned by the Strangman and Woodard families, two of Hadleigh's leading landowners.

38   Hadleigh (later Victoria) House, an imposing mansion which stood, set back, on the south-west corner of the road junction now known as Victoria House Corner. It was built *c.*1800 and was successively inhabited by several important local people, including Martha Lovibond and Sir Charles Nicholson. Later an inebriates' home, it was demolished before the Second World War.

Hadleigh House

On the main road, at the extreme western end of the parish, there was another important building—Hadleigh House. This stood, set back, at Victoria House Corner, behind where Grays Tyre & Exhaust Centre is now.

Hadleigh House was a comparatively new building, having been built for a South Benfleet landowner, Mrs. Dunlop, in *c.*1800. It had a curious claim to fame, since, despite its name, the building was actually in South Benfleet parish until a boundary realignment in the 1840s meant that its columned front porch fell within Hadleigh! It was approached by a curving driveway from a porter's lodge which stood on the main road at the staggered crossroads which preceded today's busy roundabout. It was described in 1878 as being 'pleasantly situated, commanding extensive views over the surrounding country and the mouth of the Thames'.

One of its most important early residents was Martha Lovibond, daughter of Sir Elijah Impey, Chief Justice of Bengal, who left £750 in trust in 1820 for the education and clothing of poor children in the village.

In 1828 it was occupied by the Reverend Sir John Head, at which time it had pleasure and kitchen gardens and 18 acres of grounds. It was later occupied by George Asser White Welch and also saw service as a diocesan commercial school. At the time of the Tithe Award it was owned by Thomas Brewitt but occupied by Thomas Burrells.

Perhaps its most important later owner was Sir Charles Nicholson, who acquired it in 1864 and enlarged the gardens. Nicholson found much fame and fortune in Australia, holding many important public offices, including Chancellor of the University of Sydney and Speaker of the Legislative Council of New South Wales. He was given several honorary

39 Solbys, named after its original owner William Solby, was another former Wood family property, standing on the edge of the ancient Hadleigh Common. Built in the 18th century, it survives today as private flats on the edge of what is now the John H. Burrows Recreation Ground. It occupies the approximate site of an even older Hadleigh property, Strangman Place.

degrees as well as a knighthood and returned permanently to England in 1862. He had a son, Charles Archibald, who became an architect. Charles junior worked on several local buildings, including Hadleigh church, South Benfleet parish hall and Chelmsford Cathedral.

Hadleigh House has long-since gone, but the Victoria House Corner road junction takes its name from a later name for the building. Nearby Nicholson Road and Crescent also provide a reminder of its former occupants.

Common Hall Farm

On the far side of the common stood Common Hall Farm, whose name is preserved in the current Commonhall Lane. Like Blossoms, it was owned at the time of the Tithe Award by Eleazer Tyrrell but occupied by John Pocklington. It was also probably occupied at one stage by James Tyrrell. It has long-since been demolished.

Solbys

East of Common Hall Farm, on the extreme north-eastern edge of Hadleigh common, was Solbys. Built in the 18th century and surviving today as private flats on the south eastern edge of the John H. Burrows Recreation Ground, it occupied the site of another Strangman family property, Strangman Place.

This latter building, also known as Pollingtons, was one of the principal residences of the Strangman family, who owned land in several parishes across south-east Essex, including Hadleigh, Hawkwell, Hockley and Paglesham. H.W. King traced their involvement with Hadleigh back to the reign of

Edward III and believed they could even be traced to the Norman Conquest under their previous name of Peregrinus. Their arms used to be visible in the church and King conjectured that these were destroyed by a strong local Parliamentarian contingent during the Civil War.

Although long gone, the Strangmans' old house is remembered today for its associations with probably their most famous member, the 16th-century historian, James Strangman. A one-time curate of Hadleigh, the Reverend William Heygate, wrote a novel, *Sir Henry Appleton*, in the late 1850s which included Strangman as a character and gave a detailed description of Strangman Place.

According to Heygate, the building was surrounded by a deep moat and accessed by a bridge through a gatehouse. It had a courtyard and 'a long front of low gables with timbers laid close to each other in various patterns, fringed by bargeboards of exquisite design and variety'. The windows and doors were low and the western end of the building was made of Kentish ragstone, 'with a glorious bay window at one end, filled with stained glass'. The courtyard and interior were stocked with historical items, including rood screens, reredos, tombs, memorials, fireplaces, weapons and hundreds of books. Like Morrison's account of Hadleigh Fair, Heygate's description is largely fictional but apparently based on fact.

James Strangman was a member of the learned Assembly of Essex Antiquaries and was regarded by King as 'the Father of Essex History'. He left an unfinished 'History of Essex' and several other important historical documents when he died in *c*.1595. He left no heirs though and the family died out on the death of his nephew, Robert, sometime at the beginning of the 17th century.

The building which replaced Strangman Place was originally owned by William Solby (hence the name), though it was later in the ownership of the Heber family. At the time of the Tithe Award it was owned by Jonathan Wood senior, who died there in 1860.

Bramble Hall & Garrolls

In the extreme north-east of the parish, in a remote part beyond the woods, was another important building, Bramble Hall, which has recently been demolished. It, and much of the area around here and nearby Garrolls (or Garrolds) Farm, was owned by another Hadleigh farmer, Thomas Woollings.

Other Landowners

There were also several non-local organisations which owned land in Hadleigh in the mid-19th century.

40 The *Castle* inn, one of three pubs in Hadleigh. Formerly called the *Boar's Head* and the *Blue Boar*, it benefited greatly from the increasing through-traffic in the village and subsequently had to be enlarged to cater for the growing trade. It is shown here with its old façade before the First World War, apparently captured just at the moment when an outing is getting underway.

The Dean and Chapter of St Paul's owned a cottage and over 150 acres of woodland in the north of the parish, much of which they had held since at least the 16th century. Their property probably included the now-demolished Scrub House in Scrub Lane, which was leased out to various landowners who had the right to coppice Dean and Chapter woodland in return for an annual fee. At the time of the Tithe Award it was mostly leased to George Asser White Welch. The cottage was often inhabited by gamekeepers or woodmen.

Another 70 acres of land in the parish were owned by the Trustees of Enfield Charity, including part of Hadleigh Marshes which belonged to a property called Poynetts, just over the boundary in South Benfleet.

Sion College owned over 40 acres of arable and woodland, much of it in Poors Lane. The name of this lane may well have arisen from its connections with the College, since the latter was established 'for supporting the City of London poor'.

A further 26 acres were owned by Christ's Hospital, which had a meadow called 'Place Orchard' to the north of the church and several other fields to the north-west of the village on the other side of the common. At the time of the Tithe Award their land was leased to John Pocklington.

The Dean and Chapter of Westminster owned 12 acres at Pound Wood.

The Village

Hadleigh village was becoming surprisingly active by the mid-19th century. It had pubs, blacksmiths, a butcher's, baker's and wheelwright's and numerous other businesses that had grown up to serve the needs of the small population.

Of the pubs, the *Castle* was the oldest, having started life as the *Boar's Head* in the mid-17th century and being later known as the *Blue Boar*. Like the other pubs in the village, it had benefited greatly during the early 19th century from the increase in through-trade of travellers heading for the developing

41 Hadleigh High Street, showing the *Crown* inn, probably *c.*1920s. The inn was once in the ownership of the Heber family. Note the cottages on the left—now the site of Hadleigh Library. Two well-remembered Hadleigh businesses, Lawrence's sweetshop and Schofield & Martin's, can be seen in the background.

42 Hadleigh's third pub, the *Waggon & Horses*. It apparently originated from a beershop sometime around the 1840s but its early history is sketchy and photographs of it from before the 1920s seem to show it as a house. It suffered a major fire in the 1980s and now looks considerably different from its original appearance.

resort at Southend. In 1847 it was run by John Pike, but by 1859 his wife Mary had taken over the licence. She was still licensee in 1870.

The *Crown* dates from at least the late 18th century and was once in the ownership of the Heber family. In 1847 the landlord was John Foster, whilst the pub and much of the land behind it were owned by the brewery company, Wells & Perry. By 1859 it was in the hands of a local farmer, William Emberson Benton, whose wife, Sarah, continued to be licensee until at least 1871.

The history of the *Waggon & Horses* is somewhat sketchy, though it appears to have begun in the 1840s as a beershop run by Samuel Shelley. The 'Waggon & Horses' name does not appear until later and early photographs of the pub show it looking like a house.

Apart from the pubs, the village was well served by several other businesses. George Lloyd, one-time parish clerk, was operating a baker's shop just west of the *Crown* in 1847, while Thomas Baldwin ran a butcher's just west of the *Castle*. William Doe and William Green had blacksmith's shops almost opposite Lloyd's bakery and Green apparently also ran a grocer's. The 1841 census also shows bricklayers, carpenters, dressmakers, shoemakers and thatchers living in the village, though by far the most common occupation was 'agricultural labourer'.

One of the most significant early business families in Hadleigh was the Choppen family. In 1847 John Choppen was operating a wheelwright's business in the main street just east of the *Crown* and he was soon to be followed into business by several of his sons. One son, Stephen, had a blacksmith's business, in which he was joined for a time by his brother, Alfred, whilst another son, Charles, became a wheelwright and a fourth son, Henry, a shopkeeper and baker.

By 1851 one of the best-known modern-day Hadleigh families, the Stibbards, had arrived in the village. John Stibbards was shown that year as being a sawyer, apparently living in Endway. He was the first Stibbards family member to come to Hadleigh, establishing a connection with the village which persists to this day. By 1861 he had become farm bailiff at Castle Farm, whilst his brother, Samuel, had followed in his footsteps as a carpenter. Samuel Stibbards & Sons, the Hadleigh funeral directors which Samuel founded, can trace its origins to 1867.

As the 19th century wore on, more trades continued to appear. James Carter ran a grocery business, James Ridgewell made baskets and sieves, William Smith and William Summers operated shoe repair businesses and there was another blacksmith,

43 Hadleigh blacksmith, Stephen Choppen, who served as parish constable and was later a publican. He died in 1900. The Choppens were one of the most important families in late 19th-century Hadleigh and held several important posts in the community as well as operating blacksmiths' and wheelwrights' businesses.

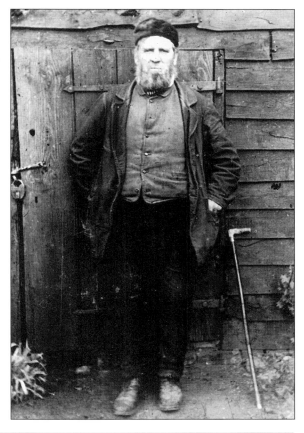

44 Stephen and Harry Choppen at the forge, *c.*1878—the oldest known photograph of a Hadleigh scene.

45   Samuel Stibbards and Sons, the Hadleigh funeral directors, which can trace its origins back to 1867 when it was founded by Samuel.

46   The village lock-up, which stood in the High Street approximately opposite where the library is now.

George Gibbs. There was even a resident surgeon in the village, William Atkinson, and there would soon be a resident tailor, Stephen Wallis. Several generations of Ridgewells operated the basket-making business well into the next century, whilst the Smiths' shoemaking business also prospered for several decades. The Raison family found much success as bricklayers.

Businessmen such as these began to replace the old farming families like the Woods and the Woodards on the parish vestry. John, Stephen and Charles Choppen all became active in parish affairs, each holding the position of parish constable, whilst Henry Choppen was a parish assessor. Stephen Choppen also held the posts of overseer and churchwarden. John Stibbards was a parish constable. Alfred Ridgewell became sexton and James Ridgewell parish constable. Roger Raison was also a parish constable, as were members of the Smith family.

The infrastructure around these businessmen was also improving. There was a Post Office, run by Eliza Benton, and a weekly carrier service to Chelmsford, operated on Fridays by shoemaker William Summers.

The increasing activity led to another notable arrival around this time—Thomas Miller, a 30-year-old police constable from Scotland, who would replace the old-style parish constables who were being succeeded all round the country from the 1840s

onwards. Hadleigh even had its own lock-up, which stood in the High Street approximately opposite where the library is now, and it also had a workhouse—in Workhouse (now Chapel) Lane—though this had closed by 1839.

The Church

With the village developing around it, the church was the spiritual and geographical centre of life in Hadleigh. Specific details of many of the earlier rectors are unknown, but the first of significance is probably Thomas Cade, who was deprived of the living in 1554 following the accession of Queen Mary—an indication, no doubt, that he was not in sympathy with her Catholic views. Cade had been rector in 1552 when one of the best surviving early surveys of Hadleigh church was carried out, listing everything that the church possessed. Items listed include a silver chalice and paten, a copper gilt cross, a white and green satin vestment from Bruges, an alb, a surplice and an altar cloth.

In 1633 John Ward was appointed rector but left just six years later to follow his father to the New World. He died in Haverhill, USA, having been born in Haverhill, Suffolk. He was briefly succeeded by Nathaniel Ward, possibly a relative.

In the 1640s, when the Civil War was raging, William Wells was rector. Clearly a Parliamentarian, he led local opposition to the King by being the leading signatory on several significant documents professing support for the Roundhead cause, which led to Hadleigh villagers being described as 'treacherous and rebellious subjects'.

In 1688 Reverend John Bromly was deprived of the living on the accession of William and Mary. A second survey of church possessions recorded a communion cup and cover, a Bible, prayer books, homilies, canons and articles, plus cloths, cushions and a carpet. The parish register was kept locked in a cupboard but this was damp and a chest was needed instead. Other items required were a common prayer book, a plate or basin for offerings, a pewter flagon for communion, a partition between the belfry and the main body of the church, new paving and a bench in the porch and a new door for the belfry.

From 1712 to 1730 Thomas Sampson was rector. His son, Samuel, held the post from 1739 to 1750.

There are a few memorials in the church which shed a little light on the lives of some of the later rectors. These include an oval-shaped tablet to Reverend William Polhill who died in 1802 at the age of 36 after 10 years as rector. His wife Jane is buried in the churchyard. Robert and John Bosanquet Polhill were also Hadleigh rectors.

At the time of the 1841 census the officiating clergyman in Hadleigh was a curate, Reverend Henry Whittington, who lived in a cottage to the west of the church. Ten years later, William Harvey was curate, though it must have been a sad incumbency for him because his son, Thomas, died in 1850 at the age of just eight months.

The services of a curate were required during this period because the rector who was supposed to be ministering to the Hadleigh flock, the Reverend John Mavor, was in Oxford—in prison!

Mavor was officially rector of Hadleigh from 1825 to 1853, but it seems unlikely that he visited his church more than once. Born in 1786 he was educated at Lincoln College, Oxford (at that time patron of the living at Hadleigh), where he gained something of a reputation for insufferability, being variously described as haughty, stubborn and temperamental. He was appointed in 1823 to the incumbency of the Oxford parish of Foresthill and two years later was also appointed to Hadleigh.

Preferring his native Oxfordshire to the marshlands of southern Essex he chose to make Foresthill his main home and appointed curates to look after Hadleigh in his absence. At Foresthill he began a scheme to enlarge the rectory, financed in part by an educational venture to train young men for a church career. This venture was a spectacular

47 A memorial tablet to Reverend William Polhill, rector of Hadleigh from 1792 to 1802. There are several similar memorials in the church to later Hadleigh rectors.

failure and Mavor was left with insufficient funds to pay for the work. He was taken to a debtors' prison in Oxford and spent the rest of his life there.

The opportunity for Mavor to leave prison did eventually arise but he is said by some sources to have been so stubborn that he chose to remain there! He was removed from his incumbency at Foresthill in 1847 but remained rector in name at Hadleigh until 1853. The Tithe Award of 1847—drawn up in the middle of Mavor's incumbency—shows the Church lands in the village to be in the hands of sequestrators.

The Enclosure of the Common

Towards the end of Mavor's incumbency, Hadleigh Common, which had for centuries been open for use to all villagers, was enclosed and parts of it were allocated to local landowners in proportion to their existing landholdings. The enclosure award was made in December 1853 and notices about the stopping-up of rights of way across old common land appeared in the *Chelmsford Chronicle*, the main local newspaper.

At the time of its enclosure the common consisted of slightly more than 47 acres, five of which were exempted from enclosure due to a legal requirement to keep part of the previously open land for ordinary villagers. Two acres were reserved for recreation and three for the 'labouring poor'. These areas survive as the War Memorial Recreation Ground and allotments on the south side of the London Road. Common Hall Lane, which runs northwards from the London Road/ New Road junction across where the common used to be, is a reminder of this lost open space, whilst New Road itself was so-called because it was a brand new road across the old common land.

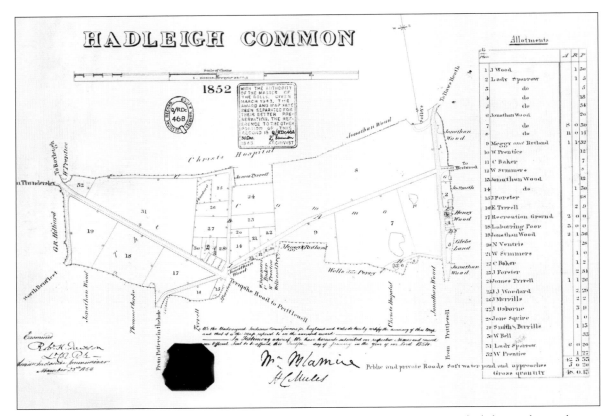

The table on the right of the map reads:

Allotments	A	R	P
1 J Wood		1	30
2 Lady Sparrow		1	5
3 do			5
4 do			18
5 do			34
6 Jonathan Wood			20
7 do	8	0	30
8 do		0	11
9 Mercy and Rutland	1	1	32
10 W Prentice			12
11 C Baker			7
12 W Summers			8
13 Jonathan Wood			12
14 do		1	30
15 Forster			28
16 E Tyrrell		2	9
17 Recreation Ground	2	0	0
18 Labouring Poor	5	0	0
19 Jonathan Wood		1	30
20 N Ventris			28
21 W Summers			9
22 C Baker		1	2
23 Forster		2	34
24 James Tyrrell	1	1	20
25 J Woodard		2	20
26 Merrills		2	28
27 Osborne		2	9
28 Jane Squire		1	0
29 Smith & Burrills		1	15
30 W Bell		0	20
31 Lady Sparrow	0	0	20
32 W Prentice		1	27
	42	3	33
	5	0	20
Gross quantity	48	0	13

48   A map drawn up in 1852 in preparation for the enclosure of Hadleigh Common, which lay to the north-west of the village centre. The main (London) road crosses the map from top-left to bottom-right. New Road—a brand new road across the old common land—can be seen running towards the top-right across the centre of the picture. The names of the individuals to whom the old common land was to be apportioned are listed on the right.

49   New Road—a brand new road across the old Hadleigh Common. It is shown here in the early part of the 20th century—note the lack of pavements and traffic. Most of the buildings in the picture survive, but the gaps between them have generally been filled.

As the common had been an important amenity for Hadleigh villagers since time immemorial, it must have been a shock to lose a freely available open space on which they had traditionally relied for the grazing of animals and the collecting of brushwood. It had also provided a recreational space for the villagers' children and was a focal point for local bonfires, including those for Fireworks Night. Gravel from the common had even been used for the repair of local roads before the highway situation had been regularised.

Benton, nostalgic for times past, wrote of how the late 18th-century common, 'then covered with furze and in a state of nature, abounding with numerous flocks of geese, and studded with tents of wanderers, appeared [to be] a scene of rural felicity'.

The loss of the common was not, however, to the complete detriment of the village. The Lady of the Manor, Lady Olivia Sparrow, who benefited greatly herself from its enclosure, gave a plot of old common land on the edge of the main road as the site for a Church of England (or National) School. The school itself cost £450 to build, financed in part by Martha Lovibond's bequest. It was built to the designs of George Edmund Street and opened in 1855. It still stands, but is now the village hall.

50 Lady Olivia Sparrow, Hadleigh's Lady of the Manor, who was awarded a portion of the enclosed common land and donated some of it as the site for Hadleigh's first proper school.

51 Hadleigh's first purpose-built schoolroom, known as the Church (or National) School and opened in 1855 on a plot of land donated by Lady Olivia Sparrow following the enclosure of Hadleigh Common. The original building has had several extensions but survives today as the church hall.

Although this was the first dedicated school building in the village, it was not the first school in Hadleigh *per se*. The earliest recorded mention of a school was in 1687, when a licence was granted to the rector to maintain one. In 1808 the curate, the Reverend Hodge, had reported that there was one day school in the village, with an average attendance of 15 pupils who were taught in reading and needlework, and after that there had been the school at Hadleigh House.

Mrs. Lovibond's trust had enabled a Sunday School to be set up at the parish church in 1820 and the rules of 'The Hadleigh (Essex) Sunday School Fund' are still preserved. The trust was to be run by the rector, who was also responsible for the appointment of the schoolteacher. The school was to operate for six hours on a Saturday (when reading and spelling were taught) and five on a Sunday (for religious teaching). Mrs. Lovibond expressed a request that the children 'should be taught to join audibly in the Church service'. There was to be no corporal punishment, but rewards were to be given for attendance and good conduct. Children were to be given a copy of the Common Prayer Book and,

on leaving the school, a Bible if their attendance had been good. At Christmas the girls were to be given a coarse straw hat and garter, blue ribbon and, once every three years, a warm grey cloak. Any surplus money each year would be put towards flannel petticoats and worsted stockings for the girls and hats or worsted stockings for the boys (younger pupils being given preference).

An inspector's report in 1836 showed that 40 children were taking advantage of Mrs. Lovibond's charity. Money was being spent on books and rewards for the children and the best Sunday School attendees were given presents at Christmas. Plans for a National (Church) School were also in the inspector's mind at this stage, though it was not until Lady Sparrow's intervention that the land became available. The early censuses show several teachers, including Maria Benton in 1841 and Sarah Lark 10 years later.

With the enclosure of the common, the first seeds were sown for the future changing shape of the village. Hadleigh would not completely change, however, until a few last links with the past had disappeared.

CHAPTER IV

Cunning Murrell

One of the most interesting 19th-century Hadleigh characters was James Murrell. Murrell, known as 'Cunning' Murrell from the widespread belief that he was a possessor of magical powers, lived in a cottage in Endway, the little lane opposite the church. He had a wife, Elizabeth, and at least 14 children, many of whom died in infancy.

Murrell was a native of Rochford, born in 1780 as the seventh son of a seventh son, but moved to Hadleigh in the early 1800s after spells as a surveyor's apprentice in Burnham-on-Crouch and a chemist's stillman in London. His official job was shoemaker, but he was known throughout south-east Essex for his ability to cure illnesses,

52 Cunning Murrell's cottage in Endway, shown around the turn of the century. Murrell, who died in 1860, was buried in the churchyard in an unmarked grave. The site of the cottages is now occupied by offices.

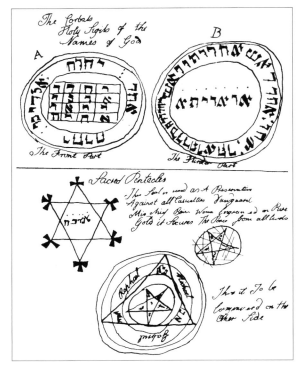

53 A page from one of Murrell's books, the *Book of Conjurations*, showing various sigils and pentacles which Murrell used to predict the future and combat witchcraft.

find stolen property and combat the forces of witchcraft.

The writer, Arthur Morrison, visited Hadleigh in the 1890s to find out the truth behind some of the legends surrounding the cunning man and wove them expertly into a superb novel (*Cunning Murrell*) that merges fact with fiction. Morrison spoke to both Murrell's illiterate son, Edward (known as Buck), and the (by then) retired village blacksmith, Stephen Choppen, who had done work for Murrell in his younger days.

The recorded extent of Murrell's supposed supernatural powers is phenomenal. He could cure people and animals of disease, chase away evil spirits, break the spells of witches and even be the master of the Devil. He knew everything there was to know, could fly through the air and could be in two places at the same time. He could travel great distances, especially at night, and his house was packed with books of all kinds, covering astrology, astronomy, botany, fortune-telling, geomancy, herbalism, magic, medicine, religion, the supernatural and witchcraft. He had various almanacs and charts, plus horrorscopes of numerous Essex villagers, and he could no doubt draw on his

training as a chemist's stillman for some of his more scientific calculations.

He was often seen out on the Downs at night collecting herbs for his magic spells and people from all over Essex would contact him, seeking help in curing their ailments, freeing them from witchcraft or returning lost or stolen property. He could predict the future, see through walls and even patch up love affairs.

There are numerous surviving stories about Murrell's accomplishments, each illustrating some magical or supernatural feat which he is said to have achieved. He was respected and feared throughout south-east Essex and beyond and was consulted by learned and knowledgeable individuals as well as by ordinary villagers. Hadleigh Post Office was said to have handled three times as many letters for Murrell as it did for everyone else put together!

One of Murrell's favourite tricks was the employment of 'witch bottles'—sealed iron bottles containing hair cuttings, nail clippings, pins and various other appropriate items belonging to an alleged victim of witchcraft that could be thrown into a fire to break the witch's spell. The bottle would hiss and explode, breaking the spell and freeing the victim.

The bottles were made for Murrell by Stephen Choppen in his forge in the High Street and Choppen later told Morrison that the practice could actually be very dangerous, with the sealed, airtight iron bottles exploding just feet away from awestruck villagers. According to Choppen, Buck Murrell had tried a similar experiment with the last surviving witch bottle after the cunning man's death and had blown out the wall of his client's house!

Another of Murrell's favourite tricks was to keep a bucket of oily fluid close to hand, which he would peer into like a crystal ball in an apparent attempt to locate lost property. On a more theatrical note, he had a telescope-like device which, he claimed, enabled him to see through walls, but which simply consisted of mirrors that played tricks with the light when the viewers put their hands between the device's two lenses. After Murrell's death, Buck sold the device to a man who later died in mysterious circumstances, with money stuck in his throat.

Several of Murrell's encounters with witches are remembered in detail, perhaps the most grisly being one involving a so-called gypsy witch. A local girl had discovered a gypsy interfering with beer stored in her barn. On being told to leave, the gypsy cast a spell on the girl, who was 'took comical'—screaming, shouting and running around on all-fours. Murrell was called for and used his tried-and-trusted

54 Cunning Murrell's chest, now on display at Southchurch Hall Museum in Southend. It was ancient even when Murrell had it and was once the storehouse of many of his magical books and writings.

witch bottle method to deal with the matter. Footsteps were heard on the path outside while the bottle was boiling away and a voice from without cried 'Stop—you're killing me!'. The bottle exploded and no more was heard from outside. The girl recovered and the following day the badly burned body of a gypsy was found by the roadside.

There are several other witch stories about Hadleigh, which may have had their origins in Murrell's activities. Perhaps one of the best known concerns a witch who lived in the vicinity of the *Waggon & Horses*. Upon her death, none of the villagers would come to lay out the body because they were all so scared of her. Her son, who had no wish to inherit his mother's powers, decided to put an end to it once and for all by stoking up a fire and throwing something live into it which he had taken from a box. Human screams were heard as the fire burned, gradually dying away until they could be heard no more.

Murrell was no doubt blessed with some genuine healing or curative powers but he also did nothing to dispel the air of mystery that surrounded him and cultivated people's fears and reverence. He claimed to be possessed with supernatural powers

and carefully timed his arrivals and departures so that he seemed to appear and disappear without explanation. He owed at least part of his success to his skill as a fanatical notetaker, writing down scraps of information about everybody in the village and using this information later to help him solve their problems and prescribe appropriate cures. Apart from his herb- and book-filled cottage, with its cobwebbed corners and table-top skull, he also dressed distinctively and was frequently seen roaming the fields during the hours of darkness, often emerging from the night to the sudden shock of an unsuspecting passerby. He kept all sorts of papers in a trunk in the corner, which he would frantically dive into when searching for information. In short, he behaved as people expected him to behave and built on his own legend every time he did so.

Murrell's nightly activities have led to some speculation that he was connected with the (declining) local smuggling industry, either through direct involvement or through his veiled warnings to villagers to stay out of the way at night while a smuggling run was going through. With its proximity to the fishing port of Leigh-on-Sea and the creek between the mainland and Canvey Island, Hadleigh

55 The only known picture of Cunning Murrell, seen looking over Stephen Choppen's shoulder during the forging of a witch bottle. The sketch was made in 1900 by artist John Louis Wimbush, friend of the novelist Arthur Morrison, from recollections of people who knew Murrell. Wimbush's other people-sketches bear a remarkable similarity to their photographs, so it is reasonable to assume that this picture of Murrell, with hard hat and thick, iron-rimmed spectacles, is a fairly close representation of his actual likeness.

offered a good landing spot for smugglers, who would bring their goods ashore at the foot of the hill below the castle and then smuggle them overland up Castle Lane, through Hadleigh village and beyond to the wild wastes of nearby Daws Heath, where items could be easily hidden from view under the undergrowth until the time came to remove them.

Not surprisingly, several smuggling legends have grown up in the area, including the claim that there was once a secret passage from the castle to the creek and that strange lights could be seen at night flashing from the castle ruins. There are stories of tunnels leading from the castle to the nearby Castle Farm, to the church and to the *Castle* inn, and the castle is even said to be haunted by its own resident female ghost, the White Lady, who is best known for her violent treatment of a local milkmaid known as 'Wry-neck Sal' after her neck was dislocated by the ghost in retribution for some offence she had apparently caused her.

Benton was extremely scathing of Murrell, describing him as an 'impostor' who played on the fears of ignorant people. 'It seems extraordinary,' he wrote, a few years after Murrell's death, 'that

this man continued his career unchecked to the end and was allowed to propogate the wildest notions.'

Later writers have tended to be somewhat kinder, buoyed no doubt by Morrison's romantic prose and the later researches of witchcraft author, Eric Maple. He has been dismissed by some as arrogant and filthy, but he was not an out-and-out fraudster, charging each customer only what they could afford. 'He would,' wrote Morrison, in perhaps the best assessment of Murrell, 'rather meddle and mystify for nothing than not meddle at all.'

Unfortunately, very little physical evidence of Murrell's existence survives. His cottage in Endway was still there in Morrison's day but has long since been demolished and, although some of his books survive, most of his letters and documents were burnt in 1956, apparently by a descendant who felt they had no value. The forge where his witch bottles were worked had gone even by the time of Morrison's visit, to be replaced by 'one of the terrible new shops' (the row of brick shops with the archway in opposite the *Castle*). Perhaps one of the best surviving items is his wooden chest, which is on display at Southchurch Hall Museum. A second chest is also thought to have survived.

As regards Murrell's appearance, there are no known photographs of him in existence, but some black-and-white drawings, penned by Morrison's artist colleague, John Louis Wimbush, from descriptions given by local people, were published in *The Strand* magazine in 1900. A sketch of Stephen Choppen in this magazine looks like photographs of the blacksmith, so the sketch of Murrell, drawn from the recollections of people who knew him, could well be equally accurate. It confirms the general view that he was a short man, with thick-rimmed circular iron glasses that made him look quite frightening, especially to children. He usually wore a blue frock coat with brass buttons and a hard glazed hat and carried a whalebone umbrella and a frail basket, in which he collected his herbs. He walked with his hands behind his back and his head in the air, humming loudly as if lost in thought. He had scrawny hands and tiny, crabby handwriting, often written in his own kind of shorthand. He spoke with a 'small, sharp voice'.

Cunning Murrell died on 16 December 1860 at 1pm, the exact date and time that he himself had predicted. Though 80 years of age, he was feisty to the last, engaging in heated discussions with local clergymen and no doubt still carrying out magic tricks and cures as long as he was able. He was buried on the east side of Hadleigh church, in an unmarked grave, alongside his wife and most of his children.

For some years after his death, Murrell's possessions were prized as souvenirs and there was a lot of interest in his life and work. There were also reports of his ghost being seen on the Downs at night, collecting herbs for his remedies. Despite a prophecy that one of his descendants would inherit them, he appears, however, to have taken his supernatural powers to his grave.

1860 is surprisingly recent for beliefs in witchcraft to have persisted, but then Essex as a county has a strong witchcraft tradition and Hadleigh was still very much a backwater. Morrison summed it up well: 'Hadleigh, thirty-seven miles from London by road, was a century away in thought and manners.'

Perhaps with the death of Cunning Murrell and the decline of smuggling, old Hadleigh also died and new Hadleigh was just beginning.

CHAPTER V

The Late 19th Century

James 'Cunning' Murrell was not the only peculiar person in the Hadleigh locality in the mid-19th century. Daws Heath, the wild wasteland just outside the northern boundary of the parish where smugglers used to hide their contraband, was home at that period to a religious sect known as The Peculiar People.

The Peculiar People

The Peculiar People movement was founded in 1837-8 by James Banyard, a native of Rochford. It took its name from a Biblical quotation meaning

that its members had been specially chosen. Banyard had been inspired to found it following a religious experience in the mid-1830s. He was already a Wesleyan, having been converted to religion after a previous life as a drunkard.

The chapel at Daws Heath was established in 1852, and Bishop Samuel Harrod, one of four leading figures in the movement, took up residence there the following year. Daws Heath (actually in Thundersley parish, but close to the Hadleigh border) had until then been a wild wasteland, a real heath which was the haunt of criminals and

56 Daws Heath in the late 1920s or early 1930s. The heath was once a remote and forbidding place, the haunt of smugglers and thieves.

57 The new rectory built by Reverend Thomas Espin in 1856. It replaced an earlier building which had been allowed to fall into disrepair by the previous incumbent, the Reverend John Mavor. It stood on the site of the current rectory and the adjacent Rectory Close is built on its grounds.

renegades. It had some history as a site for charcoal burning, but was generally regarded as a place to avoid, especially at night.

The challenge facing the Peculiar People in converting the low-life who occupied the heath must have been immense. There had already been some enclosure of the area (similar to that on Hadleigh's common) in an attempt to force the undesirables out and this must have been of some assistance to them. They introduced cultivation, redeemed several of the more desperate characters and were ultimately successful in transforming a place of hitherto bad reputation.

There was, however, soon to be a disagreement in the ranks. The Peculiars professed a belief in divine healing, which meant that when one of their members fell ill they refused to call the doctor, allowing the illness to run its course. This sometimes led to the death of the individual concerned and,

when children were involved, there was often an outcry among local people.

In 1855 James Banyard's son fell ill and, fearing that he would die, Banyard called the doctor. This blatant flouting of the rules of the sect caused a schism in the movement and Banyard was forced out; Harrod replaced him as leader and the centre of the movement changed from Rochford to Daws Heath. Banyard never regained the leadership and died in 1863.

Harrod introduced several new features, producing a hymnbook and dividing the growing movement into three circuits, but he also had to contend with more illnesses and schisms. In 1880 a new chapel was built at Daws Heath to replace the original chapel which was now too small. In the 30 years from 1855 to 1884 the movement had grown from 100 to 1,300 members! In 1891 Harrod himself was forced out following allegations about his association with a married

58 The old Methodist Chapel in Chapel Lane, erected in 1865. It still stands (on the right-hand side, behind the War Memorial Recreation Ground), but is partly obscured from view by a garage built on the front.

woman in the congregation. He was replaced by Daniel Tansley, though a strong body of anti-Tansley supporters sought for a time to reinstitute Harrod as leader. In 1894 another new chapel was erected, but with the deaths of Tansley in 1897 and Harrod in 1898 the organisation broke up into a number of factions until in 1913 the different groups were reunited.

In 1956 the Peculiar People joined the Union of Independent Evangelical Churches. Twenty years later a fourth chapel was erected as a direct replacement for the 1880 one (which stood behind it). It survives today as Daws Heath Evangelical Church. The third (1894) chapel also survives as a private residence.

Church and Rectors

After the Reverend Mavor's troubled incumbency, the position of the mainstream church in Hadleigh was in need of a lift. It got it in the form of a very able rector, Reverend Thomas Espin.

Espin, a native of Lincolnshire, was appointed to the living of Hadleigh in 1853 by the then patrons, Lincoln College. An active and learned man, he held several tutoring posts at universities and also became Rural Dean for Rochford District. One of his first tasks at Hadleigh was to institute a programme of rebuilding, with the demolition of the old rectory,

the construction of a new one and a full restoration of the parish church.

The old, largely wooden, rectory had not been occupied for several years and had fallen into disrepair, with locals carrying off its materials for use elsewhere. The new rectory, built on the same site but slightly to the east of its predecessor, was completed in 1856 at a cost of £2,000.

The parish church was also given a complete overhaul but without the overpowering Victorian zeal for restoration that blighted churches elsewhere in the county. The roof and east wall were repaired but the ancient Norman building suffered no other major structural alteration. A bonus for the restorers was the discovery of the medieval wall-paintings (see Chapter 1). They also discovered a slab commemorating Mary Beauchamp and her daughter Elizabeth, who both died in 1691.

The architect in charge of the 1855 church restoration and the building of the new rectory was George Street, designer of the church school. Reverend Espin contributed financially to all three of these projects. His gifts for the church included a new communion cup, some stained glass and an organ. The organ, which replaced an ancient bass viol, was played by the local schoolmaster and blown by one of his pupils for the princely sum of 2s. 6d. a quarter.

Espin remained in Hadleigh until 1868, when he moved to a post in Birkenhead. He was succeeded by William Metcalfe, whose father Charles had bought the advowson (the right of appointing the rector) from Lincoln College. Metcalfe, from Wisbech, stayed in Hadleigh until his death in 1876 at the age of 45 and is commemorated by a memorial inside the church. He was succeeded by Arthur Skrimshire, who served the parish until 1894.

Developments were also taking place in other churches in Hadleigh, with the introduction in 1865 of a Methodist chapel in Workhouse (soon to be Chapel) Lane. Methodism had been followed in Hadleigh since around the late 1840s, but early worship took place in private houses.

1st Edition Ordnance Survey Map

The village around the church continued to grow. The main focus was still along the High Street to the south and west, but by the time of Metcalfe's incumbency the increasing development of the old common was beginning to show some changes.

The 1st Edition Ordnance Survey map of Hadleigh (1867) reveals the extent to which this development was taking place. New Road cuts right across the old common land, whilst Softwater Lane is also beginning

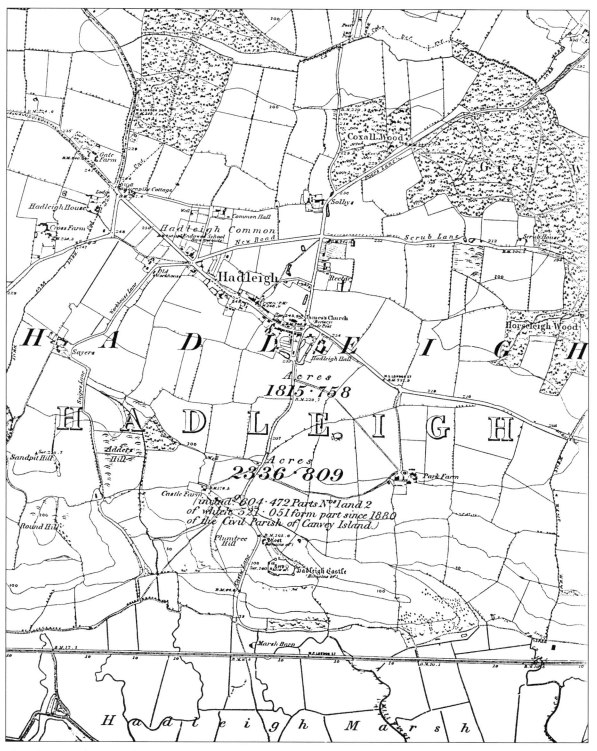

59 The 1st Edition Ordnance Survey Map of 1867, showing the beginnings of development on the old common land, including the Church (National) School. Central Hadleigh is still largely undeveloped.

60 Hadleigh schoolmaster, Alfred Hawks, apparently pictured *c*.1906. Hawks was to become one of the longest serving teachers at the Church School, as well as an overseer, churchwarden and parish councillor.

61 Charles Choppen (left), his daughter Ada and Ada's husband Alfred Lawrence, shown here celebrating the 'Good News From Pretoria'—presumably a reference to the Boer War. Charles ran a wheelwright's business; Ada and Alfred ran a confectioner's which later became known as Lawrence's sweetshop.

to make in-roads. The Church School is visible and several other buildings, including Espin's rectory, have appeared since the Tithe Award.

Overall, however, the picture is not too dissimilar from Chapman and André's map of a century earlier: woodlands still sweep in an arc around the village to the north (despite the removal of some of them to provide land for cultivation) and the land to the south is still almost entirely agricultural. Even the curving outline of the old Royal Park, to the south-east of the village towards Park Farm, can still be clearly seen.

The Church School

As the latter half of the 19th century progressed, the Church School continued to provide for the education of the village children.

The 1861 census shows a teacher, Mary Lloyd, and a 'pupil teacher', 16-year-old Eliza Pepper, who probably assisted her. By 1867 the school had a male teacher, Henry Yeaxlee, who served for 10 years from the mid-1860s.

Yeaxlee's own successor, Alfred Hawks, was to become one of the longest serving masters at the school and one of the leading lights in the village, becoming overseer, churchwarden and parish councillor over a 40-year period from the 1880s to the mid-1920s. In 1895 the original school building was extended, allowing it to cater for infants as well as juniors.

Village Life

In the 1880s Mr. Hawks was a name for the future, but there were several other traditional families still flourishing in Hadleigh.

Stephen Choppen was parish clerk throughout the 1870s and early 1880s and towards the end of this period also moved from his blacksmith's business to become licensee of the *Castle* inn. Stephen's son, Harry, became a bricklayer, whilst his brother, Charles, continued with his wheelwright's business until the early years of the 20th century. Charles's daughters, Elizabeth and Ada, ran a confectioner's and tobacconist's, which would ultimately become Lawrence's sweetshop after Ada married Alfred Lawrence.

The Stibbards family was also prospering. John and Samuel were still running their carpentry and wheelwright businesses and by the early 1870s John Stibbards had diversified into beer retailing. His son, James, became a carpenter and wheelwright and by 1891 Samuel was running a carpenter's and wheelwright's shop at Common Hall Farm, close to today's modern funeral directors.

Stephen Wallis, the tailor, married Julia, a midwife, and ran a shop in the High Street to the west of the church.

Eliza Benton ran the Post Office into her old age until the mid-1880s, whilst the Friday carrier service to Chelmsford that William Summers had provided was taken over by the greengrocer, John Havis.

At the *Castle*, Joseph Binder succeeded the Pikes as licensee before Stephen Choppen took over. Binder served on the parish vestry, as did one of his successors, John Cracknell, who was of great assistance to Arthur Morrison in his researches about Cunning Murrell.

At the *Crown* James Francis became landlord and, like his colleagues at the *Castle*, also opted for a life of public service, becoming overseer, surveyor and parish councillor. Both pubs also operated pony and trap hire businesses.

One of the largest landowners in Hadleigh in the 1870s and 1880s was Major Thomas Jenner

62 The grave of James Swaine Potter, one of Hadleigh's most successful late 19th-century businessmen, who was a grocer, draper and master baker. At his death in 1891 he was living in Hadleigh Hall.

Spitty, who had purchased much of his land from Lady Olivia Sparrow. The Spitty family owned land in neighbouring South Benfleet parish, including Great Tarpots, and had traceable ancestry in other parts of the county, notably at Billericay, Great Burstead and Rettendon.

One of the most important businessmen to emerge in the latter half of the 19th century was James Swaine Potter. A native of Hockley, he found much success in Hadleigh as a grocer, draper and master baker, with premises between the *Castle* inn and Endway. He succeeded Eliza Benton at the Post Office and even lived in one of the old Hadleigh properties—Hadleigh Hall. He became parish clerk, overseer and parish assessor and was churchwarden for 30 years. He died in 1891 and was buried in Hadleigh churchyard.

Another important individual to appear at this time was Henry Charles Buckenham, a butcher and cattle dealer, who lived for a time at Blossoms. He became overseer and assessor. Many other local businessmen took an active part in Hadleigh affairs during this period, including Thomas Woollings, Thomas Ellis, Frederick Manning, Talbot Hart,

Peter MacKay, Dr. Robert Bakewell, Henry Law, Alfred Gilliat, James Low and various members of the Snow and Sivell families.

Calm before the Storm

Despite this increasing business activity, the population of Hadleigh had remained static for centuries. The road through the village had seen more traffic as time went on and the railway had encouraged more travellers, but most of them passed the village by. Those that did discover it, inspired to do so by the lofty towers of Hadleigh Castle which overlooked the railway line which brought them to the area, did so only as daytrippers, taking a four-penny carriage ride from Leigh station and walking back across the downs via the castle on their return.

Even in the 19th century, a time of great expansion elsewhere, the village population hardly changed. In 1891 the total population of Hadleigh was just 526, an increase of barely 200 over the previous 80 years.

Within a decade, however, the population was to expand beyond all expectations, following the arrival of the Salvation Army.

CHAPTER VI

The Salvation Army

The Salvation Army was founded in 1878 by 'General' William Booth, a preacher from Nottinghamshire who felt pity for outcasts and a hatred of dirt and squalor. He founded a Christian Mission at Whitechapel for the care of the poor and destitute in the Capital and the Salvation Army evolved out of this Mission.

Booth's new organisation gained its military-sounding name from the fact that its rules, regulations and organisation were modelled on the British Army, complete with the designation of ranks such as 'general' and 'major' for its leading figures. The ethos behind it was based loosely on the 'Cab Horse Charter'—a belief that, like the working horses in London, every human being should have food to eat and a roof over his head.

The Army's first meetings were often controversial, with violent local opposition. There were fights and riots at many of them and Booth and his supporters were often jailed or fined for breach of the peace. By 1890, however, opposition to the movement had quietened and feelings of antagonism were gradually replaced by a certain sympathy for the cause.

Booth's plans for his new organisation were outlined in his 1890 publication *In Darkest England And The Way Out*, written in collaboration with a London newspaper editor and journalist, William Thomas Stead, and incorporating the views of a more radical salvationist, Frank Smith, who was later to resign from the organisation. The ideas outlined in Booth's book included a scheme to rescue the poor and destitute from the squalor of London, train them in agriculture and general farming practices and then either find them jobs in Britain or provide them with the opportunity to go abroad to work on the vast open spaces in British colonies such as Canada, Australia and New Zealand.

The Farm Colony

To carry this scheme through, Booth needed to purchase a large area of farmland on which those he was rescuing could work. He was happy to take any land he could get his hands on, ranging from existing under-used or unproductive farmland to overgrown railway embankments. His intention was to run a proper farm—a Farm Colony, as he called it—and he set about the task with enthusiasm. 'My present idea,' he wrote in 1890,

> is to take an estate from 500-1,000 acres within reasonable distance of London. It should be of such land as will be suitable for market gardening, while having some clay on it for brickmaking and for crops requiring heavier soil. If possible, it should not only be on a line of railway which is managed by intelligent and progressive directors, but it should have access to the sea and to the river.

63 General William Booth, founder of the Salvation Army, seen here on a tour of inspection of the Hadleigh Farm Colony.

July 30, 1892.   THE WAR CRY.   3

A DAY ON THE FARM.

THE FIELD COMMISSIONER SHEPHERDS A GIGANTIC FLOCK
O'ER COLONY "PASTURES NEW" AND TO THE SOUL'S "STILL WATERS."

"Beautiful weather. Little rain yesterday. Ground dry."

That was the wire which the Field Commissioner made it her business to send off to The General almost before she had marshalled her first train full of light-hearted London soldiers out of Leigh Station and formed them up before the eyes of the astonished townsfolk, last Monday morning.

Sunday's rain, so steady and drenching in London, had fallen lightly, it would seem, over Hadleigh Colony, for the Field Commissioner's motherly fears lest her gigantic flock should find muddy roads, dripping hedges and damp grass, were far from realised. Bright sunshine fell on jubilant faces, where, aided by Majors Higgins and Lawrence, with a host of London and Garrison staff, she formed a ring at the Church Corner and began an open-air which lasted while the second, third and fourth trains were unloading their two thousand five hundred excursionists.

Then Major Wright, the Farm Governor, came galloping up, and the Commissioner mysteriously disappeared, to join her first contingent as it met the second and lead them, as mounted marshal, on their two-mile march up the New Road to the Colony.

"Miss Booth," said one sturdy soldier, "I love to look at you on a platform, but I can't look at you on that horse. I'm so afraid you might get hurt!"

"How good it is of my soldiers to love me when they hardly know me," said Miss Booth, almost tearfully, to one of her staff. "They smile at me where'er I pass. They are good—good to me when I am all new, and have done nothing for them yet."

Yet our blessed soldiers' hearts do not need long acquaintance to learn to love those who come to them in the name of the Lord, and the Commissioner's passing seemed to bring a fresh flicker of sunlight upon them wherever she moved, hunting up a delicate-looking officer to stow away in one of Major Wright's waggonettes, or pointing out the way to the refreshment stall to a tired, hot group.

Once on Colony grounds, the hundreds seemed a marvellously small number. They scattered over the broad acres to study the piggeries, which we saw the Field Commissioner with three Majors passing in solemn review; or to watch the rabbits; or to inspect the brick-making, just as fancy and curiosity led them. The crowd was lost. The press and noise one associates with the word "excursion" were absent. No better place for a Salvationist pleasure party could be conceived.

"Everybody seems delighted," said Mrs. Wright to us, "and the word 'wonderful' is the one almost commonest among them."

Major Wright had made the most of his opportunity for disposing of Colonial products. Pots of currant and raspberry jam, leaves full of red raspberries, tiny glass jars of honey, &c., were sold at every turn. The new refreshment-room, built on purpose for the accommodation of excursionists, was crowded all day. The Colony officers were busy everywhere in attending to the wants of their London comrades, except for those to whom fell the direct supervision of the three hundred Colonists themselves. It was not a holiday for the Farm men, but Miss Booth insisted that they must stop work at four o'clock and come to the meeting. So by four o'clock hilarious little rows of them might have been seen leaving the fields in all directions, their hoes over their shoulders, splitting their throats with shouts of "Fire a volley for the Field Commissioner!" "Three cheers for the Field Commissioner!"

The Colonists seemed to enjoy our visit very much, even though they were bombarded in all directions.

"What are you doing in that box?" asked a

SALVATION IN THE CASTLE COURT.

London officer, popping her head into a curious wooden structure situated on the roadside.

"Keeping time," was the answer.

"Are you saved?"

"Yes, bless the Lord!"

"How long?"

"Six weeks!"

"Glory to God, keep true!" and the head was withdrawn.

"I suppose these visitors look at you all very hard!" said the Governor's wife to one of the Colonists who came to her house on an errand during the course of the day.

"Yes, they do," answered the Colonist; "they have been staring in at us while we had our dinner, and we don't care about it."

"Oh!" said Mrs. Wright, sympathisingly, "I suppose you did not care about people watching you at your meals!"

"It is not so much that," said the man, with a touch of beautiful Colonist pride. "Only we didn't have such an extra dinner to-day, and we didn't care about them seeing it. If it had been a day when we had those big beef-steak puddings, now, they might look all they liked! But it was only beef and beans."

This dear fellow's spirit of loyalty to the Colony seemed to pervade all the men and showed more satisfactorily than anything else would have done that they are getting to feel just that sense of self-help and proprietorship in

Colony matters which will be their best education.

At half-past three, Majors Richards and Higgins began to collect the congregation for the meeting at half-past four, and at four the Field Commissioner set out for her curious

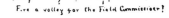

Fire a volley for the Field Commissioner!

open-air auditorium, inviting people to come with her, right and left, as she passed.

"Where are you going, Bandmaster Appleby?" she cried, as she met that redoubtable musician, apparently heading in the wrong direction.

"Going to fetch the band, Commissioner," was his enigmatical answer, as he sped breathlessly on.

What he might mean was a mystery. But the Field Commissioner walked on, past the big red and white sign of the Trade Headquarters, under which rapid officers were selling books and bonnets and tambourines, up the Castle Hill, and round to one side of the crumbling towers of the old fortress. There, in the old castle court, the great meeting was waiting, sipping

The land was to be freehold and sited 'at some considerable distance' from any town or village. This latter requirement was essential because Booth considered, with some justification, that alcohol was one of the principal causes of the downfall of the men he was trying to save and that the lure of any nearby public house might be too great for them to resist.

Booth and his colleagues looked at several locations for a Colony, before settling on one at Hadleigh.

The Army arrives in Hadleigh

On 25 March 1891 a deposit was paid on the purchase (for £12,000) of 800 acres of farmland at Hadleigh, later increased to 3,200 acres and incorporating the three farms on the Downs to the south of the village—Castle, Park and Sayers Farms. Formal possession was taken on 2 May and a notice was put up announcing that the land had been purchased by the Salvation Army 'for the establishment

of the first Farm Colony and elimination of the "submerged tenth"' (Booth's description of the poor and destitute).

The challenge was immense. Much of the land they had purchased had been left fallow for years because of the difficulties of cultivation and was known locally as 'the badlands'. Much of it was also steep-sloping and did not lend itself well to cultivation. On top of this, Hadleigh village, though some little way to the north, did have public houses—a possible thorn in the side of the scheme.

Most significantly there was much opposition from Hadleigh people. Many local residents, who had for centuries lived a fairly undisturbed existence, did not take kindly to the idea of having a 'colony of rascals' as their neighbours. They feared fights and thefts and general unruliness and in the early years there were several disagreements between Army staff and parish representatives. The Army tried unsuccessfully to get its officers elected to the

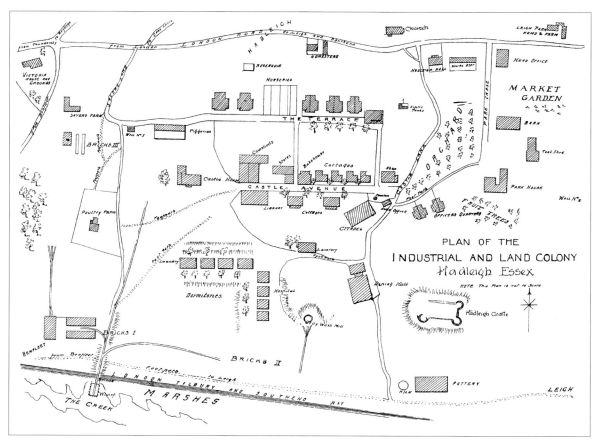

65 A map of the Salvation Army's Farm Colony, c.1900, showing the extent of the Army's possessions and some details of the activities which took place there.

parish council and there were numerous disputes over rights of way across Army land. One newspaper was particularly scathing, describing Booth as 'Baron of Hadleigh'. 'The paths to the castle are … to be shut up against the public unless they pay Booth tax,' the paper told its readers, 'so that no blackberrying is to be done there now except by the Salvation Army. Thus a source of income to the cottagers of the parishes of Hadleigh and Leigh is to be cut off and diverted to the tumid pockets of General Booth.'

In practice, however, there was little the villagers could do and, in the end, many of them came to be thankful for the Army as it offered them employment which could never otherwise have been expected.

The Scheme in Detail

There were several major advantages of the Hadleigh site. The three farms together offered a massive area of cultivatable land and there was good road and river transport. The latter provision was particularly important as Booth intended to build a wharf below the castle (also in Army ownership) and use barges to transport materials to and from his rescue centres in London.

One of Booth's most far-sighted themes was recycling: manure from London horses would be used to fertilise the land; old scraps of tin would be converted into toys and sold to raise money; and grease and fat from London slaughterhouses would be used to lubricate farm machinery. Barges from London would bring the raw materials, whilst the return journey would enable transportation of farm produce direct to the Capital's markets.

With hard work, the Colony quickly prospered. By the end of 1891 there were over 200 Colonists on the site, plus Army officers and various other employees. Existing farm buildings were converted and new buildings erected. Dormitories, a kitchen, a bathroom, a laundry, a dining room, a reading room and a hospital were all introduced, together with a Citadel—the place where religious meetings were held.

The extent of Colony activities rapidly grew. A Colony Governor was in overall charge, whilst superintendents looked after the different departments beneath him. There was crop farming, livestock, poultry, market gardens, orchards, a brickworks, a pottery, a wharf, a dairy, allotments, workshops, glasshouses, provision stores 'and all the elements of an industrial and agricultural community'. There was even shire horse breeding, beehives and a rabbit warren!

The Colony was a master of self-sufficiency. Its middle white Yorkshire pigs were 'the pride of the farm', while the Army's fruit-growing activities were pioneers in south-east Essex, with much of the open field on the London Road to the east of Hadleigh being covered with fruit trees. Some of these innocuously survive, tucked away in subsequently developed corners of old Army land, such as in the central reservation of nearby Sutherland Boulevard.

By 1896 *London* magazine could report that the Colony was flourishing. 'Where weeds once grew,' its reporter wrote, 'there is now one of the finest market gardens in England.'

One of the most ingenious parts of the scheme was a tramway linking the three farms to the Colony wharf. There were steep hills to be negotiated and a special elevator mechanism was introduced to enable the trucks to cope with the gradients. The brickworks in particular benefited from this tramway—millions of bricks were made and transported. The tramlines have long-since gone, but the remains of a brick bridge which took them over the main London-Southend railway line can still be seen.

Colonists on the farm were subject to a strict system of progression, as they gradually proved themselves willing and capable. Leigh Park Farm, another Army acquisition on the main road to the east of Hadleigh village, was used as a 'receiving station'— a Colony in miniature—where prospective Colonists were assessed for their willingness to work and the seriousness of their intention to be 'saved'. From there they progressed to the Colony proper, where the best workers were rewarded with the most responsible jobs and the best sleeping arrangements. Although Colonists did not get paid, they were given grants of money for the work they did and the grant increased as they gradually proved themselves. It was very much a system of reward for achievement. There was also a Colony 'coinage'—a system of tokens which could be exchanged for purchases— which gave the Army some control over what the Colonists spent their money on.

Expansion

As the scheme developed, the Army bought more land and property. One later purchase was Hadleigh House and it was they who renamed it Victoria House—the name which survives in today's busy roundabout junction.

Victoria House's location away from the centre of Hadleigh was a big selling point for the Army. Some distance from the village's public houses, it was ideal as a home for inebriates, which the Army

66 The entrance to the Farm Colony, just before the First World War. Castle Farm farmhouse can be seen in the distance. The road to the left leads down to Hadleigh Castle.

67 The wharf at the Farm Colony was an integral part of General Booth's scheme, since it enabled both the landing of raw materials and the transportation of produce by river to and from the Capital. The Colony's internal railway system ran right onto the wharf, allowing for easy loading and unloading of barges.

68   The dormitories at Hadleigh Farm Colony. Colonists worked their way up from basic accommodation to more luxurious surroundings as they proved their worth on the surrounding land.

69   The poultry farm—one of the many facets of Farm Colony activities.

70 The work of the Colony was centred around agriculture. This ploughing team is seen at work on the field which abuts the London Road to the east of Hadleigh. (Modern-day Tattersall Gardens is away to the right.)

hoped to cure of their addiction to drink. The establishment opened in 1901 and about twenty to twenty-five 'inmates' were kept there, with a 60-70 per cent abstinence success rate.

Another Army purchase was a large part of the Hadleigh Hall estate, which came up for sale in the early 1890s. The Hall itself was used as the Colony governor's residence, though in later years the governor lived at Park Farm. The Army also purchased the old Blossoms farmhouse in Hadleigh High Street, which they renamed The Homestead.

They also bought Place Orchard, a meadow to the north of the church (which may once have belonged to Strangman Place), and by 1895 were the largest landowners in Hadleigh.

With its many facets, the Farm Colony attracted numerous sightseers and a refreshment room was built near the castle to cater for visitors. A photographic studio was later attached to it to enable visitors to have their photos taken on-site and Park Farm was sometimes made available for visitors to stay in.

By 1903 a school had opened for the Colonists' children, but it soon began to attract villagers' children as well. By 1905 it had approximately 100 pupils, some 60 per cent of them from the village.

Later on, Local Boards of Guardians sent paupers from their parishes to the Colony, paying a subsidy to the Army in return for their employment on the land.

The Colony at its Peak

Shortly after the turn of the century, men from the Colony were being sent abroad in large numbers to put their training into practice in the colonies. By 1905 the scheme was so successful that H. Rider Haggard (Commissioner and novelist) came to see it for himself and report on progress.

Haggard considered that the Colony 'might prove useful as a training ground for the managers of settlements [overseas], or of industries, such as brick-making and carpentering, which will be practised in them'. He was, he wrote later, 'much interested and impressed by what I saw there'.

Haggard was not the only well-known visitor. Henry Chaplin, President of the Board of Agriculture, had already been there, as had the Honourable Cecil Rhodes and Sir Walter Besant. Even

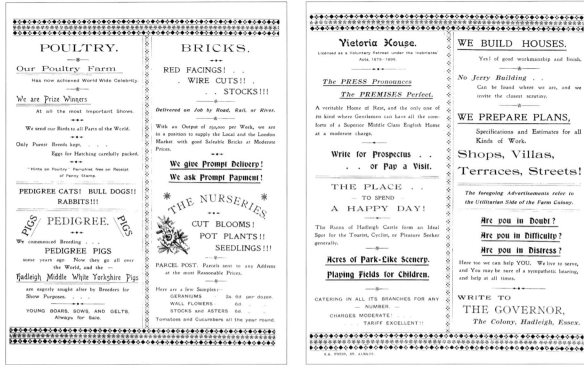

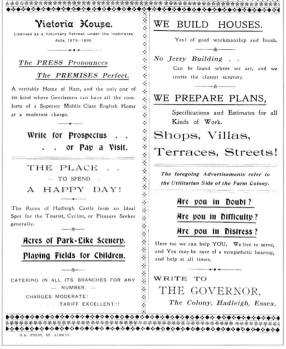

71 & 72   A selection of advertisements taken from a book of the Colony which was written just after the turn of the century. The range of activities covered is staggering!

Queen Victoria was buying produce from the Army's farm!

Representatives of a Royal Commission into poor laws and relief of distress also visited the Farm Colony and reported very favourably on it. The men, they noted, 'work with an energy that was refreshing to observe'.

Problems

The Colony had made fantastic progress, but there were nevertheless some problems with the scheme. General Booth had hoped it would be fully self-financing through sales of its produce and the renting out of land, but every year since its inception it had made a trading loss. It had, of course, made many other non-financial gains, such as the rescuing of hundreds of destitute and poor people, but there remained the harsh reality that it could not continue to lose money. It often took three Colonists to do the work of one experienced farm labourer and the overheads were consequently considerably higher than had been expected. The Colony could never be financially viable whilst its workers came from a class of downtrodden and comparatively unskilled men,

working on poor quality soil which had itself failed to live up to expectations.

By 1912, its 21st anniversary, almost 7,000 men had passed through its gates, the vast majority of them going off successfully to new 'situations' elsewhere. The days of the original Colony ideals were, however, numbered—the coming of war would be the final straw.

A Changing Role

The First World War and its years of senseless slaughter led to a shortage of men throughout the Kingdom. Some troops, including Belgians, were sent to the Colony for convalescence, but the net post-war reduction in the numbers of young men, combined with an increased emancipation of women and the need to rebuild the nation, led to a revision of the country's social structure. The role of the Colony had also to change.

The railway and brickfield operations were scaled down, some of the outlying farmland was sold off and the size of the estate was reduced to around 900 acres. Much of this land was subsequently built on, but a reminder of its Salvation Army origins can still be found in the deeds of many local houses, which forbid the making or selling of alcohol.

THE COLONIST

Published for our own pleasure and instruction

Nº 6   February 15 1892.   Gratis

As Others See Us.

The "Weekly Bulletin".

a journal of Finance, Mining and Instruction says:-

"Still in Essex as I write these lines. To-day I have walked mile after mile through a district yet unknown to me & always the same sad, sad tale. Field after field un-tilled, house after house fallen or falling to pieces. Farms that afforded existence & happiness to generation after generation, all tumbling to pieces, and as to cottages, many of the roofs (Even when they are, inhabited) are open to the daylight. Ah God! can such things be?

But stay– what is this? Impossible. My vision must be mad- dancing mad! What do I see or think I see? I scarce dare look; but yet surely I do see men & carts and horses, and new gates and clipped hedges! And hear whistling, whistling, ye gods, and songs – why, I never such in Essex before! But my eye travels on and on, and true or not seems to embrace within its vision hundreds nearly of acres of cabbages, or wurzels, or turnips, or vegetation of one sort or another with dozens or scores of ablebodied men, laborers or non-laborers but all at work somehow! And now that I am nearer I see buildings of every description erected, or in course of erection I see the fields are ploughed- yes, actually ploughed, and I dance as I hear the dear old whistle of an agricultural steam engine. But what does it mean? At the moment I ask myself this question, I see close & a notice board that

---

73 The only known copy of the Colonists' own newspaper, dating from 1892 and published at Park Farm. Handwritten by the Colonists themselves, this edition includes letters asking the Colony Governor to provide a new clock and enquiring whether Colonists could become Salvation Army officers. There was also a report that a new kitchen was nearing completion.

74   An aerial view of the Colony brickworks in 1931.

By the early 1920s the Colony had broad-ened its operations to include training 'in rudimentary land crafts' for boys. Carpentry, house painting, boot repair, laundry work, cooking and general household skills were all taught and within a few years some 3,000 boys had been accom-modated, many of them later going abroad to put what they had learned to use in British colonies. Some unemployed men were also still being catered for, but not in the vast numbers of the pre-war period.

From the 1930s onwards the Colony's activities began rapidly to decline. Some youngsters were accommodated there in the late 1930s whilst escap-ing the Spanish Civil War, but during the Second World War only a few people who were not fit for military service were sheltered there. Much of the army's land was temporarily requisitioned by the military, with anti-aircraft guns and searchlights being erected on the Downs.

After the Second World War, which led to further social reforms and, significantly, the intro-duction of the Welfare State (where people could claim benefit without having to do any work in return), the Army's role at Hadleigh changed again. With fewer down-and-outs and an increase in

75 Remains of the brick bridge which once took the Colony tramway over the main London–Southend railway line to meet the barges at the wharf.

76 Leigh Park Farm, one-time receiving station where prospective Colony workers were assessed for suitability before being put to work on the Colony proper. The farmbuilding survives but its land has been developed as part of the Highlands Estate.

77 A home for inebriates was set up by the Salvation Army in the old Hadleigh mansion, Hadleigh House. It was renamed Victoria House by the Army—the name survives today in the road junction, Victoria House Corner. This picture shows some of the inebriates who were looked after there.

state-sponsored health initiatives, the days of the old-style Colony were over.

By the early 1950s there were two superintendents running the Colony, one looking after the farm and the other the market gardens. The two roles were eventually combined in the early 1960s, though there was still nominally an Army Commissioner in charge of the Colony until 1969.

Another post-war change was the training of probation and ex-borstal boys on the farm, whilst the numbers of alcoholics and homeless people accommodated had rapidly decreased since the First World War. A gradual transition was underway from Colony to commercial farm.

By the end of the 1960s the social side of the work had virtually ceased and the farm was being run as a commercial undertaking, with profits being ploughed back into Salvation Army funds for use elsewhere. It was not, however, until the 1970s and 1980s that this really got going.

Today

The Salvation Army's relationship with Hadleigh has gone through many changes since its arrival in the village. Where once several hundred men

78 The Colony experiment attracted several sightseers and the Army set up a refreshment room near the castle to cater for this interest.

79 By the 1920s the role of the Farm Colony had changed and the focus was more on the training of boys 'in rudimentary land crafts'—something which would prepare them for a new life overseas in British colonies. This party left Britain for Australia in 1926.

80 West View, built by the Salvation Army to house farm Colonists. The building survives but is currently unused.

worked on the land, the three Army farms are now run by one farm manager and a handful of employees. As technology has advanced, men and horses have been replaced by tractors and combine harvesters.

The Army currently farms 928 acres. The undertaking is run from the old Castle Farm, now known as Home Farm after a name-change by the Army, and its principal crops are wheat, barley, beans, rye, oil-seed rape and potatoes. Beef cattle are also kept there. Profits made by the farm are ploughed back into the Army's other ventures, which still include giving food and shelter.

Several changes to the farms themselves have also taken place. The old Castle Farmhouse, dating from the early 18th century, gradually began to fail the test of Time and was demolished in the 1970s. West View, a house at Castle Farm built by the Army to house Colony inmates, now stands empty. Various other Army buildings, such as those connected with the brickworks at Sayers Farm, also survive. Park and Sayers Farm farmhouses are

both still in Army ownership, but do not form an active part of the current enterprise.

Perhaps one of the most interesting links with the past is the modern day Training Centre at Home Farm, which recaptures in spirit at least some of the aims of the original Colony. Opened in 1990 by 'General' Eva Burrows, the Centre provides opportunities for those with special training needs, ranging from the mentally or physically handicapped to ex-offenders and the long-term unemployed. Training is provided in computing, catering and carpentry, whilst general education in life skills (form-filling, budgeting, shopping, etc.) gives trainees a good grounding in basic needs for life in the modern era.

One of the most poignant reminders of the Colony can be found in Hadleigh churchyard, where a special area at the eastern end contains the graves of Colony officers and workers.

The Colony might be dead, but the Salvation Army as a religious organisation is still very much alive in Hadleigh. Its band is a popular entertainment throughout the area and the Army

81 The Salvation Army band, around the time of the First World War. The band featured musicians from many local families. Those pictured here include Jack Barber (4th from left, in white jacket) and Arthur Barber (very back row, right-hand side).

Temple in the High Street hosts all kinds of services and meetings and provides in various ways for community needs. The Temple owes its origins to a difference of opinion in Army ranks in the late 1930s, as retired officers living in the village could not face the walk down to the Colony Citadel for their weekly services, so a separate and additional place of worship was provided. As the Colony began to decline, the Temple became the main place of worship. Retired officers are still accommodated in Hadleigh—in a specially-built row of bungalows in Florence Gardens.

In 1891 the arrival of the Salvation Army was to prove a major catalyst for change for the sleepy backwater village. From then onwards, Hadleigh would never be quite the same again.

CHAPTER VII

Out of the Dark Ages

With the arrival of the Salvation Army, the foundations were laid for Hadleigh to begin a fairly rapid, if somewhat reluctant, transition from a backwater village into a small country town. The Army and its Farm Colony attracted more people to the area and the gradual sell-off of farming estates such as Hadleigh Hall and Blossoms provided land which could be developed for housing. Traffic to Southend was increasing and the roads and general infrastructure would soon have to be improved.

Hadleigh Hall Estate

The arrival of the Salvation Army coincided with the death in 1891 of the local businessman, James Swaine Potter. Potter's home, Hadleigh Hall, was acquired by the Army for use as their Colony governor's residence, but much of the farmland belonging to it was sold off for development.

Castle, Ash, Oak, Beech, Branch, Elm and Short Roads were laid out on old Hall land to the south of the London Road, whilst Church, Meadow, Bilton, Seymour, Broughton, Woodfield (part) and Alma Roads, plus The Avenue and The Crescent, were laid out to the north and east. The line of Castle Road mirrored the line of the boundary between the Hadleigh Hall estate and Park Farm, thus preserving the ancient boundary of the old Royal Park.

Shops were provided on many of the development plans for the estate but most were never built. 'Taverns' were also planned, but conditions of sale imposed by the Army meant that no premises which made or sold alcohol could be built on their old land. A plan for a hotel at the junction of London Road and Horseleigh Road (a lost lane to the east of Alma Road) also fell by the wayside. Development to the north of Woodfield and Alma Roads was checked (for the time being) by Horseleigh Wood. Many of the new houses were built of bricks made at the Salvation Army's brickfields.

Lynton Estate

Another area earmarked for development in the early 1890s was the Lynton Estate, to the west of the village near Victoria House. In 1892 149 plots were laid out in Lynton, Fairlight and St John's Roads, the latter being marketed as a 'new direct approach to the village' (since it linked the estate with Chapel Lane). St Mark's Road was also laid out at this time. Shops were planned for St John's Road, though again the developers' 'tavern' plans fell by the wayside.

The estate agent's sales pitch for this estate gives a good guide to what made it marketable, though

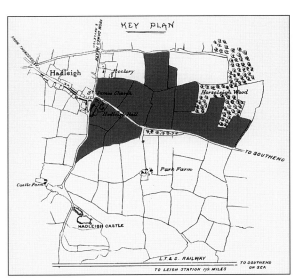

82 A map showing the extent of the Hadleigh Hall Estate at the time of its sale in 1891. The whole area was laid out for development and many new roads sprang up where previously there had been only fields. The curving line to the south of the Hall marks the old north-western boundary of the Royal Park. Development to the north-east has been checked—for the time being—by the presence of Horseleigh Wood.

LYNTON ESTATE
HADLEIGH, ESSEX.

Particulars, Plan, and Conditions of Sale

OF

FREEHOLD BUILDING PLOTS

Adjoining with Frontages to the Road from Benfleet and other Roads formed through the Estate, commanding Splendid Views of the Kentish Hills, the River Thames, and a large expanse of open country.

MESSRS.

TALBOT & WHITE

WILL SELL BY AUCTION,

IN A MARQUEE ON THE ESTATE,

On THURSDAY, the 28th Day of JULY, 1892,

At 2 o'clock p.m., about

150 PLOTS OF
FREEHOLD BUILDING LAND

Being a PORTION of the

LYNTON ESTATE, HADLEIGH,

Situate about 1½ miles from Benfleet Railway Station, affording easy communication with London and Southend at very low rates, and

ADMIRABLY SUITED FOR RESIDENTIAL PURPOSES.

Possession given on completion of 10 per cent. Deposit; Balance by 16 quarterly payments. Free Conveyance will be granted.

A DISCOUNT OF FIVE PER CENT. WILL BE ALLOWED TO ALL BUYERS PAYING CASH WITHIN TWO MONTHS FROM THE SALE.

Return Railway and Refreshment Tickets, 2/- each, will be issued by the Surveyor and Auctioneers to intending purchasers by the Train leaving Fenchurch Street at 11.30 on the morning of Sale. The Refreshments will be provided in the Marquee.

Particulars, Plans, and Conditions of Sale may be had of S. G. Goss, Esq., Surveyor, 42, Poultry, in the City of London; Messrs. McDIARMID & TEATHER, Solicitors, 5, Newman's Court, Cornhill, London, E.C.; at the "Crown," Hadleigh; "Crown Hotel," Rayleigh; at the "Ship Hotel," Leigh; at the "Headley Arms," Warley, Essex; and of the AUCTIONEERS at their Offices, High Street, Southend-on-Sea.

WARNE & SON, Printers, 127, Upper Grange Road, Old Kent Road, S.E.

83 An advert for the sale in 1892 of building plots on the new Lynton Estate. The development of estates like this and Hadleigh Hall paved the way for the rapid growth of Hadleigh village.

84   A bungalow on the Lynton Estate. The estate was marketed as being approached by one of the loveliest drives in the Home Counties, sheltered from north winds and within easy walking distance of Southend!

some of the claims are a little extravagant. 'This beautiful estate,' ran the advert,

> is favourably situated within easy walking distance of the rapidly growing seaside resorts of Southend and Leigh-on-Sea ... approached by one of the most lovely drives and walks which are to be had in the Home Counties ... From North winds it is sheltered by extensive woods which makes Hadleigh and Benfleet noted for its high degree of temperatures in the coldest winters ...

2nd Edition Ordnance Survey Map

The best pictorial representation of the expansion generated by the sale of Hadleigh Hall is provided by the 2nd Edition Ordnance Survey map of 1896 which, though only a few years after the commencement of development, already shows a dramatic change to the road layout of the village.

This period of expansion was the first planned mass development in Hadleigh's history and it was ultimately to transform completely the appearance of the one-time backwater village. From 1891 to 1901 the population of Hadleigh almost trebled, from 526 to 1343.

The Parish Council

With a growing population and an increasing need for an infrastructure to support it, the village must have welcomed its next major change—the introduction of the parish council.

Initiated by an Act of Parliament in the mid-1890s, parish councils were introduced across the country as a replacement for parish vestries. Hadleigh's council was established in December 1894 and the village was simultaneously incorporated under the next tier of local administration, Rochford Rural District Council. Elections were held in December 1894 and the first meeting took place at the Church School on 1 January 1895.

Many of the councillors in the first few years were already of some status in the community. They included Alfred Hawks (its first chairman), James Francis, John Stibbards, Charles Choppen, Stephen Choppen, Henry Buckenham, Talbot Hart, John Marks, Stephen Faux, John Faux, William Abbott, Frederick Eyre and George Richards. Charles Judd, one-time overseer, became a long-serving parish clerk. Several of the early councillors also went on to serve on the Rural District Council and even on the County Council. They included Herbert Mitchell (a former parish chairman), Henry Robinson and Bird Samuel Porter.

Virtually from the start, the new council found itself at odds with the Salvation Army, usually regarding disputes over rights of way across Army land. In March 1895 the Army was obstructing rights

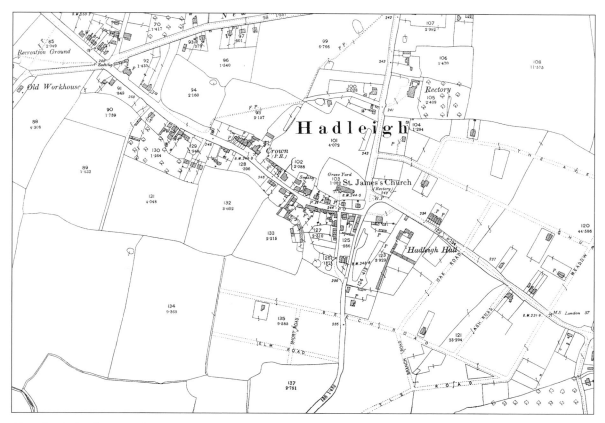

85 The 2nd Edition Ordnance Survey Map of central Hadleigh in 1896. Note the new roads laid out on the old Hadleigh Hall Estate to the south and east of the village. The 1890s was the first period of planned mass development in Hadleigh's history, something which was destined to change irreversibly the physical shape of the village.

of way with its refreshment room and tramway. The following year it had barred access to its pond in Place Orchard. Further problems arose at Sayers Farm and on the Saddleback, with parish councillors actually walking the footpaths to see if they would be challenged. A request to the Army to repair a stile in 1908 was met with the response that the Army 'deny the existence of a right of way over the Saddleback and therefore do not feel called upon to facilitate trespass'.

The council frequently sought help in resolving these disputes from Rochford Rural District Council and even Essex County Council, though usually to little effect. It can have come as no surprise to the Colony governor, Colonel Lamb, when, in 1907, the parish council decided not to support his nomination as a district councillor—and it must have been even harder for the parish council to secure District support when Lamb was actually elected!

It was not just the Salvation Army that was giving the council problems. One of their most

frequent complaints was about the state of the roads and, in particular, the dangerous nature of the highway at Hadleigh (Hall) Corner (immediately east of the church), which took the form of a sharp 'S'-bend. Complaints about road conditions had been made for many years and by 1907 the 'many motors which daily pass' had combined with the poor road surface to make Hall Corner one of the most dangerous spots in the village. The preferred solution of widening the road relied upon the Salvation Army selling part of the frontage of Hadleigh Hall—and the Army was not in the mood to sell. In 1910 the construction of some shops at the Corner compounded the problem and the following year councillors wrote to the County Council that 'owing to the immense and increasing motor, cycle and vehicular traffic, this Parish Council would draw special attention to the dangerous condition of Hadleigh Corner near the church and it is hoped that the County Council may make some improvement before a serious accident happens'. It was not,

86 The late 1890s and early 1900s saw several local disputes between the Salvation Army and the parish council, particularly about rights of way. In 1906 the dispute boiled over and many of the Army's newly erected fences were cut down. This picture shows both the Army's attempt to obliterate a signpost and the villagers' response in cutting down its fences.

87 Four of the Salvation Army's earliest Farm Colony governors, pictured *c.*1905. Colonel Lamb (bottom right) exchanged several letters with the parish council during the early disputes between the two organisations.

GOVERNORS, PAST AND PRESENT, OF THE COLONY.

88 The sharp 'S'-bend at the east end of the church (known as Hadleigh Corner) gave the parish council much cause for concern in the early years and contributed to several motor accidents in the village. The shop in the background, Jonathan Webster's butcher's, was one of Hadleigh's best-known pre-First World War businesses.

however, to be until the 1920s that something was finally done about the situation.

The road problems were having a knock-on effect on other council resources. In June 1911 councillors put in a request for an additional police officer, because 'on Sundays and throughout the season the present officer is forced to be on point duty at Hadleigh Hall Corner to prevent accidents'. Some highway improvements were, however, made, including the tarring of most of the main road through the village and the making-up and kerbing of pavements.

Perhaps because of the dangerous state of the road, the council was an enthusiastic supporter of a tramway scheme to connect it with Southend and wrote to Southend Town Council asking for their support. In 1909 it pledged to 'do all in its power to further the promotion of the tramway scheme'.

By this stage there was already a cab stand in the village, at Hadleigh Corner, where the traditional method of travel to and from Leigh was by 'Hadleigh Fourpenny', a horse-and-cart ride from Hadleigh church which cost fourpence. Nevertheless,

89 The Cingalee Tea Gardens. The construction of new premises here at Hadleigh Corner caused much consternation for the parish councillors in the years before the First World War since it led to reduced visibility and increased the likelihood of road traffic accidents. The road in the distance is Rectory Road. The churchyard is behind the cottage on the left.

90 The Hadleigh Fourpennies, Hadleigh's earliest 'taxis', in a picture dating from before the First World War. Named after the cost of the fare from Hadleigh to Leigh-on-Sea, they congregated at the east end of the church to ply for trade. Some of the buildings to the left of the church have survived, but the road here is considerably busier now.

91 Hadleigh's first bus (note the 'Leigh' destination nameplate at the front and the formally attired conductor at the rear). The date of the picture is uncertain, but is thought to be *c.*1905.

the council was well aware of the need to look for alternative modes of transport and in 1911 it responded positively to an idea from Commercial Car Hirers Ltd to provide a 'Saloon Motor Bus Service' to Leigh, with special desire expressed for a direct link between Hadleigh and Leigh churches.

The council often showed a genuine concern for the welfare of Hadleigh people and in 1908, when Leigh Urban District Council began to make changes to the way it issued licences for conveyances on hire to and from Hadleigh, councillors wrote to express their concern that Hadleigh drivers should not be disadvantaged.

In 1907 the council decided to petition the Great Eastern Railway (G.E.R.) for a railway station to be provided on the marshland below the castle, giving as one of their reasons that 'considerable development has taken place within the last few years whereby the population has greatly increased'. The G.E.R. was amenable to the council's request, with the condition that the council provided an approach road to the station—a road that would have to cross Salvation Army land. The council wrote hopefully to the Army asking if they would be prepared to

provide such access, but can hardly have been surprised to receive, in March 1911, a reply stating that 'the advisers of General Booth cannot recommend him to go to the expense of a railway station'. The railway scheme for Hadleigh was effectively dead.

By 1911 Rochford Rural District Council was beginning to recognise its own needs to expand and sought the parish council's help in putting its case for the acquisition of new urban powers which would enable it to make-up roads and lay sewerage pipes. The parish council was very much in favour and was happy to report in July 1912 that the District Council had had its request granted.

There had already been several improvements to the local infrastructure by this stage, with water supply, sewerage, lighting and gas all on the agenda. The parish's stance on water was particularly interesting, councillors feeling from the outset that it was sufficiently supplied by springs and wells as not to necessitate the expense of a piped supply. Several times in the 1890s they exchanged letters about it with the District Council. They felt so strongly, they were even prepared to overlook their differences

92   The entrance to Rectory Road at Hadleigh Corner, with the church out of the picture on the left. This area, where the Hadleigh Fourpennies congregated and where villagers met and exchanged their news, was historically the focal point of Hadleigh village. The building in the background is still there, but the rest of the scene has changed completely.

93 An amazing photograph of the section of main road to the east of Hadleigh Church, known as The Broadway. The houses in the distance are now shops, the buildings in the foreground have been replaced by car showrooms and the road itself now throngs with traffic.

94 The Broadway from the opposite direction. All the houses here have now been converted into shops and the front gardens have been lost to road-widening and pavements.

95 Castle Lane, looking south, between Endway and Beech Road. All the houses in the picture have survived, but several properties have appeared alongside them.

96 Further down and on the other side of Castle Lane from the previous picture, this photograph shows Edmund Hylton's Tea Rooms, which was a popular stop for locals and visitors on their way to the castle. The Salvation Army buildings at Castle Farm can be seen in the background. The building stands on the north corner of the junction with Castle Road and is now a private residence.

97 The High Street, *c.*1910. The cottages on the right stood in front of the church. Blossoms, the old double-roofed farmhouse, can be seen in the distance. The *Castle* inn—on the left in the middle-distance—is the only recognisable building today.

98 Listed here as 'High Road' and sometimes called The Causeway, this is the London Road to the west of Hadleigh fire station where there is now a dual carriageway. The brick building in the centre is the *Waggon & Horses*, but the three houses on the right have been demolished and the site is now occupied by Safeway's carpark.

99 The crossroads at Victoria House Corner (now replaced by a roundabout), leading to Canvey (to the left), Tarpots (straight on) and Rayleigh (to the right). The building on the left was the lodge of Victoria (formerly Hadleigh) House—the entrance gates to the house grounds can also be seen.

100   Pupils of the Salvation Army's Colony school, *c.*1903. The headmaster, Major Collins, can just be seen on the extreme right.

with the Salvation Army, preferring to use an Army well to a District-imposed piped supply.

The resistance lasted until October 1901, when the District Council finally had enough of the matter and wrote to tell them that they were having a new piped water supply whether they liked it or not. By June 1911 208 houses in Hadleigh were connected to the water mains and not long after that the council was sufficiently enthusiastic to be actively seeking a transfer of its suppliers from the District Council to the Southend Waterworks Company.

Within five years of a decent water supply being implemented, councillors were seeking to link to Leigh and Southend's sewerage system, but sewerage was to prove one of the banes of the council's life and arguments about it raged on until the mid-1930s.

Gas, too, was an early bone of contention, the council noting indignantly in its minutes in 1912 that the County Council had instructed a gas company to lay mains in the village without informing them in advance. The company had left several trenches open 'at great public inconvenience'. In later years, however, the council was to work closely with the Grays & Tilbury Gas Company in providing, amongst other things, considerably better streetlighting for the village.

Streetlighting had been discussed as early as 1907, but it took until 1912 for a scheme to go ahead. An

advertisement in the paper that year invited tenders for the maintenance of the council's 12 streetlamps, initially powered by oil, later by gas.

There were many other matters for the council to resolve. A flooding pond on the highway at Solbys caused particular problems and the matter was not resolved until the pond was filled in. In November 1897 'the clerk was directed to ask PC Totterdell to endeavour to prevent loafers from congregating at the corner of Chapel Lane, especially on Sundays' and in 1906 the council received a letter from the coroner asking them to inform residents that it was dangerous to bathe in Benfleet Creek.

The New Council School

Perhaps one of the most contentious matters under discussion in the early years of the 20th century was education.

In 1907 the Board of Education wrote to the council asking them to investigate the possibility of providing a new Council School to meet the needs of the growing population. The old Church School was still in existence and had been supplemented since 1903 by a school on the Salvation Army Colony. The Church School had already been enlarged and the Board was clearly concerned that it was not meeting residents' needs.

Fearing an increase in rates if construction went ahead, the council told the Board that it thought the

To the Right Hon. the President of the Board of Education ;

To the Essex County Education Committee ;

And to all others whom it may concern.

The Essex Education Committee having under public notice, dated the 30th Oct., 1907, announced their intention to build a Public Elementary School for the Parish of Hadleigh and the Daws Heath portion of Thundersley, in the County of Essex, we, the undersigned Ratepayers of the Parish of Hadleigh, object to the building of such school, and hereby appeal to the Board of Education to decide that such proposed school is unnecessary, and before coming to any decision to hold a local Public Enquiry, at which your Petitioners may give and call evidence shewing, among other matters, that—

(a) There is already ample accommodation for all the school children of the district served by the schools situate in the Parish of Hadleigh.

(b) That with such alterations and improvements as the Foundation Trustees of the Church of England and Salvation Army Schools respectively are understood to be willing to make, the existing schools ought to be regarded as reasonably satisfactory.

(c) That the County Medical Officer and the County Architect have visited the Salvation Army School and did not condemn it.

(d) That there are less residents in the Parish of Hadleigh than there were at the taking of the census of 1901.

(e) That any school or schools in the Parish of Hadleigh must necessarily serve, in addition to Daws Heath, the South-Eastern Portion of Thundersley and the North-Eastern Portion of South Benfleet, and therefore the area for which it is proposed to provide the school should be enlarged.

101 The text of a 1907 petition sent to the Board of Education objecting to the construction of a new school in Hadleigh. The objectors' claim (d)—that there were fewer residents in the village than in 1901—would not seem to be entirely truthful!

village's educational needs were being admirably met by existing schools. They even offered the Board a visit to the Army school—with its 'playground equal to any in the whole county'—in an attempt to persuade them. The Board remained unmoved,

replying that it was 'not in favour of continuing the present arrangement as to the Colony School indefinitely'. The council set up a petition which received widespread support, but the Board would not back down and by March 1910 the new Council School was under construction. The Salvation Army school continued to operate until the Council School was completed. The Church School soldiered on until the mid-1920s when it was finally merged with the Council School and the old school building became the parish hall.

Business

With the support of the parish council, much of the work of constructing new Hadleigh buildings went to local people, notably Samuel Stibbards and the builder, Lewis Upson. A new row of shops (the ones which Arthur Morrison found so unappealing) was built in 1900 as a visible sign of commercial expansion.

The original Post Office was taken over by Emma Potter and a second office in The Broadway (as the section of main road to the east of the parish church was now known) was also introduced. There was a lending library, run by Samuel Church, and by the start of the First World War there was even a Telephone Call Office in the village.

Dr. Grant became the village doctor, operating from premises near Victoria House Corner, and, apart from the inebriates' home provided by the

102 The new Council School in Church Road, shown shortly after its construction in 1910. The building survives as Hadleigh County Junior School. Note the unmade road!

103 The new (1900) row of shops in the High Street, which opened up new opportunities for Hadleigh businessmen and provided extra choice for Hadleigh residents. George Wayland Potter was a well-known businessman. One of the village's best-known later businesses was Dossett's bakers, who later had the shop on the other side of the archway.

Salvation Army, there was also a private institution at Bramble Hall. Apart from his medical duties, Dr. Grant is also thought to have been the first person to drive a car in Hadleigh.

The Sheavill family succeeded the Cracknells at the *Castle* (and were destined to be landlords there for several decades), and James Francis continued to run the *Crown* until the First World War.

Jonathan Webster, Theodore Attwell, Ernest Smith and George Wayland Potter all ran butchery businesses (Potter doubling as a grocer), whilst perhaps one of the most prominent businessmen in the early years of the century was Arthur Yeaxlee, son of the former schoolmaster, who established a profitable drapery business almost opposite the *Castle* inn. He was also a churchwarden for many years. Other businesses of note included Heathcote's bakery and Hadleigh's first bank, Capital & Counties.

The Church

At the church, Reverend Skrimshire had long since been succeeded by another Metcalfe, Armine George, who was to serve the parish from 1894 to 1905. Metcalfe himself was succeeded by Douglas Adamson, incumbent from 1905 to 1925.

This pre-First World War period also saw the arrival of the Congregational Church in Hadleigh, with a small hall for worship being erected in 1903 on the corner of Rectory Road and Church Road. The first services were held there in January 1904 but the movement grew so rapidly that a new larger building was soon required.

The First World War

This period of rapid growth and prosperity was tempered a little by the coming of the First World War which brought some changes and minor hardships. The parish council received several complaints

104 Emma Potter's Post Office in Hadleigh High Street—now the Conservative Club. The Post Office later moved down nearer to the church before ending up in its current position in Rectory Road. Most of the cottages in the background are still there, though one is now a Volkswagen motorshop and one has been demolished to allow access to the Catholic Church behind.

105 One of the delivery carts seen about the streets in early 20th-century Hadleigh—Smith the butcher's.

106 Arthur Yeaxlee was one of many businessmen who benefited from the opportunities provided by the growing Hadleigh village. He is seen here in a pony and trap, c.1905, with his son Maurice, and, apparently, the boy's nurse, Martha Snow.

107   Heathcote's bakery.

108   F. Outen's greengrocer's and general stores. Heathcote's and Outen's were two of Hadleigh's early businesses.

109 An incredible photograph, *c*.1905, of the site at Hadleigh Corner now occupied by Iceland, Midland and Barclays. The Congregational Church (on the right) is the only recognisable landmark. The area between the church and the photographer has long-since been developed with shops and houses.

about 'the reckless manner in which motor lorries conveying munition workers to and from Kynocks [a weapons factory] are driven through Hadleigh village'. As early as November 1914 the parish also found itself playing host to a large number of con-valescent Belgian soldiers, whose collective health was evidently improving so rapidly that the parish council felt obliged to apply to the police to tighten up the local licensing hours! In March 1917 the Rural District Council told a somewhat piqued parish that it had nominated several plots in Bilton, Seymour and Woodfield Roads for the growing of potatoes for the war effort. Councillors also took exception to the establishment of a communal kitchen in the village which 'is not, and never was, necessary'.

The recognition of the need for 'protection from fire caused by aircraft' also prompted the formation of a Volunteer Fire Brigade, the parish's first serious attempt at establishing a fire service. In June 1915 £75 was made available for firefighting equipment and hoses, canvas buckets, a handcart and scaling ladders were all purchased. Colonel Simpson, a member of the parish council, was made

110 A close-up of the Congregational Church (now the United Reformed Church), *c*.1920. Despite a few alterations over the years the building is still recognisable, though it cannot now be seen from this angle following the construction of houses on the land in the foreground.

111 Hadleigh's first Volunteer Fire Brigade was established during the First World War, following the threat of fire caused by the dropping of incendiaries. It was, however, to be several years before the village got a fully functional fire service. This picture dates from *c.*1928.

112 The war memorial on the recreation ground, dedicated in October 1922 and seen here shortly afterwards.

captain and the equipment was stored centrally at Hadleigh Hall. Simpson played an active role in the local war effort—he was also a leading member of the Special Police Force.

When the war was over, thoughts turned immediately to celebration and numerous ideas were floated. In November 1918, in the hiatus of success, it was proposed that 'a grand procession will be held through Hadleigh on the day of Peace Proclamation [and] the Kaiser (in effigy) will be carried in his coffin and afterwards publicly hanged and burned'. Whether or not this extravagant celebration actually took place is unclear, but a bonfire and fireworks display definitely formed part of the celebrations, being held in the meadow near the *Crown*.

A war memorial was also erected, a suitable obelisk being unveiled on the recreation ground at a dedication ceremony on Sunday 15 October 1922. The parish church contains another memorial, as well as one to a specific soldier, 19-year-old chorister Stanley Haves, who was lost at Ypres in 1917.

The war had caused a pause in Hadleigh's development. Once it was over, the process of development would continue again at full speed.

113   The war memorial in the church porch.

CHAPTER VIII

Between the Wars

Continuing Development

The inter-war period saw yet more rapid growth for Hadleigh. The process of development set in train by the sale of the Hadleigh Hall Estate continued throughout other parts of the parish, particularly in the east. Here, pressure for development from within combined with pressure for westward development from Southend and several new roads were created on old Salvation Army farmland. Leigh Park Farm was swallowed up by housing (though the farm-house itself has survived) and the new Highlands Estate appeared out of nowhere on the boundary with Leigh-on-Sea.

Other new estates were developed. Hall Cres-cent, Arcadian Gardens and Beresford Gardens were laid out to the north-west of Commonhall Lane, taking development to the edge of the hitherto re-mote West Wood. The old turnpike cottage was demolished and, in central Hadleigh, the ancient Blossoms estate (renamed The Homestead by the Salvation Army) was sold and new roads (Homestead Road, Homestead Way and Homestead Gardens) appeared in its place. Victoria House also disap-peared under development, being replaced by Hadleigh Park Avenue and some shopping frontage.

Templewood Road, Dalwood Gardens and Cen-tral Avenue all appeared and even Poors Lane, a backwater in a backwater at the best of times, began to sprout offshoots, such as Orchill Drive.

Between 1920 and 1928 400 new houses were built in Hadleigh, bringing with them 2,000 new inhabitants and swelling the village's population to over 3,500.

The pace of this expansion is well illustrated by a comparison of the 1922 and 1939 Ordnance Sur-vey Maps. The 1922 picture might look developed compared with previous maps, but it is nothing compared with the 1939 one.

Perhaps the most significant sign of progress, however, was a new road—a bypass for the old Hadleigh High Street—which cut right through the heart of the village.

114 An amazing photograph of Woodfield Road, *c.*1920s, before wholesale development transformed the area.

115 Victoria House Corner during the inter-war period. The Lodge from picture number 99 has survived (along with one of the gateposts), but shops have appeared on the old mansion's land where it abuts the main road.

A New Bypass

The clamour for some kind of traffic improvement had been going on since the 1890s. The parish council had done its best to bring the problems at Hadleigh Corner to the attention of the Rural District and County Councils, but with little success. The construction of the Council School (and its attendant children) had brought further concerns and the council had begun to campaign for a 20mph speed limit through the village.

By the early 1920s the message appeared to be getting through. The police and the A.A. both lent their support and the County Council agreed to press the case for a speed limit with the Ministry of Transport. In 1921 the parish council, supported by petitions from tradesmen, told the County Council that 'no other length of road in the whole district is so dangerous, so narrow and so crooked'.

The County Council's solution was to construct a brand new road to the north of the church which would bypass the old High Street completely. It was built in 1924 on land owned by Wells & Perry and the Salvation Army.

Welcome though it was, the bypass did not solve all the problems and there were two accidents on the new road itself within the first few months. The parish council continued to press for a speed limit in the old High Street, this time of just 10mph, and was even in favour of introducing a one-way system (just like today's) which would take London-bound traffic through the old High Street and Southend-bound traffic along the new bypass. They pressed the County Council and Essex Police about it, but the Chief Constable replied that there was no legislation in existence to stop drivers driving where they wanted and, in any case, the new road had been built to take traffic out of the old High Street and the police were not about to encourage it to continue to use it.

Public Transport

The construction of the bypass at least made it possible to introduce some improvements to the road junction at Hadleigh Corner and the opportunity was taken to build a new bus stand on a triangle of land outside the eastern wall of the church where the horse-drawn Hadleigh Fourpennies had formerly waited.

By now public transport was motorised and there was fierce competition going on between rival bus

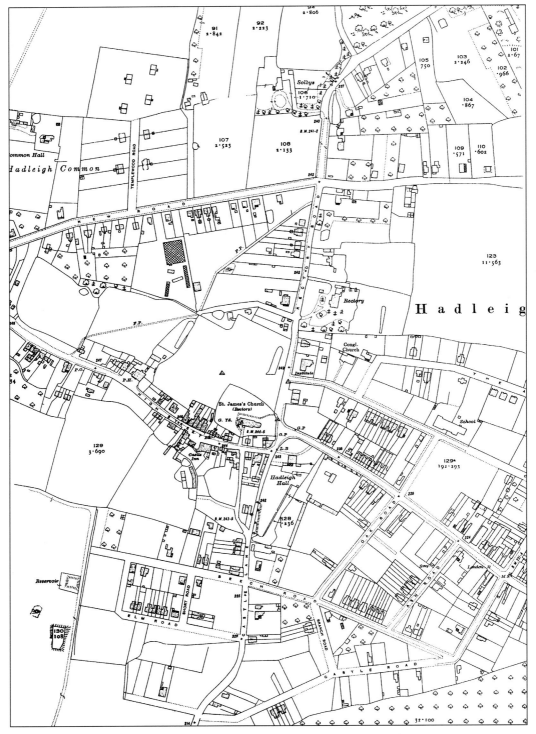

116   3rd Edition Ordnance Survey Map, 1922

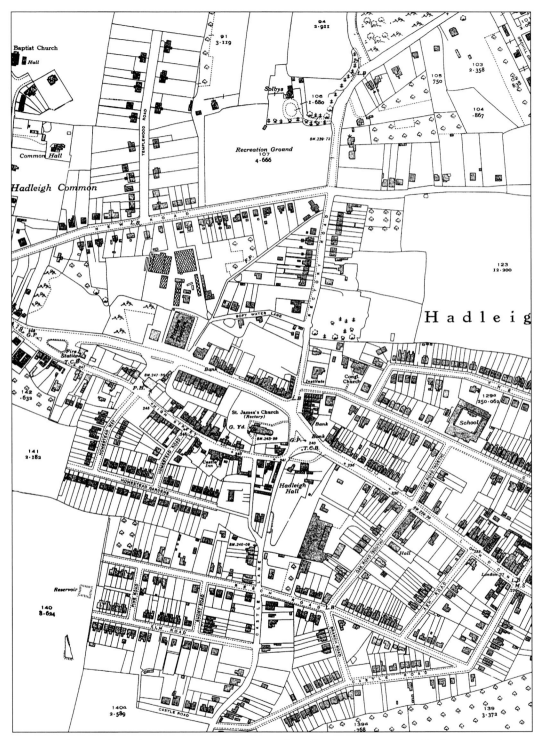

117 The large-scale Ordnance Survey Maps of central Hadleigh in 1922 and 1939, shown together to illustrate the extent of development which took place between the wars. Note the new road on the 1939 map—a 'bypass' for the old High Street—which cuts right through the centre of the village.

118 An incredible Edwardian photograph of Rectory Road, looking south, shown here to illustrate the change that the new bypass would bring to Hadleigh. Buildings in the old High Street can be seen in the distance. The new bypass would cut right through the hedge where the lady is walking. This area is now occupied by shops and a carpark. Only the church and churchyard have not been substantially altered.

119   The new bypass from the east.

companies. One of the largest was Westcliff Motor Services which operated routes throughout south-east Essex. Their rivals for a long period were the Bridge family, whose Edwards Hall Motors sought to open up new routes for passengers who lived in areas not served by Westcliff. Hadleigh, which sat astride the main east–west route, found itself caught up in the battle.

The history of bus travel in south-east Essex throughout this period was one of mergers, takeovers and frequent births of new, often short-lived, companies. One of the companies absorbed by the growing Westcliff outfit was Thundersley, Hadleigh & District Motor Services, which had its own garage in Rectory Road (thanks to a takeover

of Hadleigh Motor Bus Company in 1919) and another at Oak Road South which was used for repairs and engineering. This offered villagers a frequent service to Leigh church and connections to Southend's tramway network, as well as providing regular services to Benfleet railway station and Rayleigh.

After some harmonisation in the late 1920s, the Westcliff and Bridge family disagreements broke out again and in 1932 the Bridge family set up another new business, Benfleet & District Motor Services, with its own garage in London Road near Victoria House Corner. The company lasted until 1951 when it was sold to the British Transport Commission, but the garage has survived and

120 The new bypass from the west

121 The third of three pictures of the new bypass. The first two come from the lens of the renowned Essex photographer, Fred Spalding, who often deliberately captured moments of change in the county and appears to have done so here as the road looks as if it has only recently opened (making them *c*.1924). The third picture is slightly later as shops have begun to appear. The development land being marketed on both sides of the road in the third picture was quickly filled with shops.

122 The Triangle at Hadleigh Corner in the early 1930s, created following the development of the new bypass (out of the picture on the right). The Hadleigh Fourpennies have been superseded by motorised buses but the focal point for waiting customers has not altered. (The church is on the right behind the trees; the narrow road in the background is Castle Lane.)

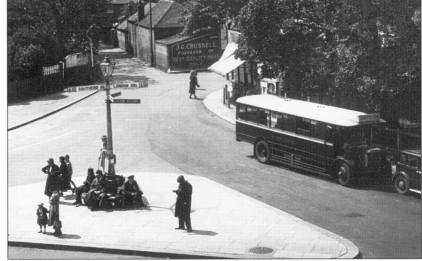

123 Rectory Road from Hadleigh Corner. The garage on the right, which stood approximately where Iceland is now, was originally part of the public transport bus network, being home to the Hadleigh Motor Bus Company and its successors Thundersley, Hadleigh & District Motor Services. It was, however, later used as a commercial garage.

124 The Oak Road bus garage—home to Thundersley, Hadleigh & District Motor Services before their takeover by Westcliff Motor Services.

is now in the ownership of Thamesway. The old Thundersley & District garage in Oak Road South is now a car showroom and workshop.

Other Issues

Roads and transport were not the only long-standing issues occupying the parish council. The campaign for a decent sewerage system was still dragging on and several acrimonious exchanges took place with the Rural District Council about it. In 1925 it was recorded that 'Hadleigh Parish Council are so seriously concerned with the way the sewerage work is being carried out in Hadleigh that they wish to lay their case before the District Council as a matter of urgency'. Different schemes to link up with Benfleet and Southend were discussed, Hadleigh being consistently in favour of a Southend link, feeling that the lie of the land was such that its sewers would drain naturally into the Southend system without too much expense.

The construction of the Highlands Estate provided the final impetus for the completion of a system

125 Another view of Thundersley, Hadleigh & District Motor Service's Oak Road bus garage (*c*.1920s), this time seen from The Broadway. The company's fleet was generally known as 'The Red Buses', a name which can be seen on the sign over the door. The houses on the right are now shops; those on the left have been replaced by Maplin Electronics. The garage itself has been replaced by a car showroom.

126 Councillors of the first Benfleet Urban District Council (1929-30), including several Hadleigh men who had served on the old parish council.

BENFLEET URBAN DISTRICT COUNCIL. 1929-1930.

W. JOHNSON. FIRE BRIGADE	C. W. GRUBB.	A. C. REMNANT.	P. LANDGRAF.	T. J. EVANS. J.P.	H. P. KRUSE.	E. J. JEANES.	H. A. W. YEAXLEE.
W. H. SHEPHERD. C. C. FIRE BRIGADE	C. J. LEGGETT.	L. H. HERRING. SANITARY INSP.	Dr. N. LORRAINE. M.O.H.	G. W. BOOTH. SURVEYOR	D. A. MELLIAR. RATING OFFICER	G. PEACE. LAW	L. J. RIVETT. FINANCE
J. M. LITTLEJOHN. ALLOTMENTS	W. A. BINGHAM. TOWN PLANNING	B. S. PORTER. GEN. PURPOSES	F. W. BURGE. CLERK	A. R. ADAMS. J.P. CHAIRMAN	G. W. HEARD. VICE CHAIRMAN	H. J. FOWLES. HIGHWAYS	H. R. TUTT. PUBLIC HEALTH

127 The new shops on the bypass.

which had been several years in the making, as the westward spread of Southend finally brought its infrastructure in touch with Hadleigh's. Nevertheless, the completion of the system was not without its problems and there were frequent complaints from residents about the inconvenience caused by the construction work and many rows about who was paying for it.

With sewerage sorted, the only thing missing from the infrastructure was electricity. As early as 1924 the Thundersley & Benfleet Electric Light Company had written to the council asking if they could be of assistance, but councillors decided not to take any action. Within three years, however, they were approaching the Rural District Council to get electricity installed and work was well underway by the end of 1929.

The End of the Parish Council

Since before the First World War the parish council had been making overtures to Southend about joining that authority and there had been numerous other discussions about union with other parishes, including Thundersley, South Benfleet, Rayleigh and even Eastwood. Throughout the 1920s the feeling that some kind of union would take place grew stronger, both within the parish and without, and

the only questions now seemed to be not if there would be a union, but when, and with whom.

Several meetings took place with neighbouring authorities and throughout the discussions Hadleigh was consistently in favour of a union with Southend (no doubt attracted by its working sewerage system and the prospect of linking to the rest of its infrastructure). This often put it at odds with its neighbours. In 1927 councillors wrote to Southend asking to join them, but were turned down.

Meanwhile, Essex County Council was pressing ahead with proposals to link the village with Benfleet and Thundersley in a new three-pronged urban district. The option had been discussed in the past but was not one which the parish council favoured and councillors wrote several times to the County asking them to consider other options.

In 1928 a conference was held between all the authorities involved and Hadleigh sent four representatives along. They were immediately accused by other parishes of wanting to link with Southend without giving other options due consideration. They promptly withdrew.

It was now only a matter of time and by the end of the year the County Council had approved a union with Benfleet and Thundersley, to take effect from October 1929. The parish council took one

128 Another view of the shops on the bypass. G.J. Keddie & Sons has become sufficiently established by the time of this photograph to be known simply as 'Keddie's', whilst the transformation of the shed-like 'Estate Office' into the imposing 'Estate House' provides a visible symbol of the progress being made in the development of the village.

129 Arthur Yeaxlee's old shop in the High Street (now the Ancora Restaurant). Yeaxlee was one of several businessmen who transferred to the new bypass to make the most of the passing trade.

130 Dossett's the baker's delivery cart. The man on the left is Joe Grant, who ran a smallholding connected with Dossett's in Scrub Lane (roughly where Greenacres is now).

131 The Broadway, looking towards the church, which is obscured by the trees. The premises on the right are no longer residential and J.P. Ross' shoe repairers has evolved into a dental surgery. The bus shelter (centre left) has disappeared and the road has been widened.

last swipe at its new partners, writing to the Benfleet council that it did not want any of its 'objectionable' industrial areas on Hadleigh territory, but in practice there was little it could do. From now on, Hadleigh would be under the control of the new Benfleet Urban District Council.

Several Hadleigh councillors went on to be leading lights in the new Urban District, including: Bird Samuel Porter (a future chairman of the new authority); Henry Reginald Tutt (another future chairman and a long-serving headmaster of Hadleigh's Council School); Eli Jeanes (a future vice-chairman of the Urban District Council); George Heard (former chairman of Hadleigh Ratepayers' Association); and Edgar Mundy (who was noted for his strong views about several local issues).

Business

The construction of the bypass had opened up more street frontage and the north side of the new road opposite the church was quickly developed with new businesses. G.J. Keddie & Sons took the prominent corner site at the junction with Rectory Road and men like Arthur Yeaxlee moved their businesses from the old High Street to the new bypass. Businesses like the *Castle*, which could not practically

move, were enlarged. The Sheavill family was still at the helm at the *Castle*, whilst another long-serving publican family, the Ellisons, had taken over the reins at the *Waggon & Horses*.

More familiar names also began to appear. Lloyds, Barclays and Westminter Banks all opened offices and the London Co-operative Society also appeared. Light and service industries emerged and the estate agency business grew rapidly to fulfil a growing need.

Other well-remembered businesses from this era include the Attwood family's cycle and photographic shops, Bellsham's Post Office and general stores, Lawrence's sweetshop, Batchelor's and Dossett's bakeries, Brackin's Dairies, Schofield & Martin's chain store, The Boot Box shoe repairers, Porter's general store, Johnny Flatt's outfitters & general stores, Gower's cycle shop, Drakard & Co. corn merchants, Norman's cycle and wireless supplies, Crussell's butchers, Levitt's fishmongers, Owen Brothers' greengrocers, Matthews & White's grocers and Howard's Dairies.

One of the most interesting characters of the period was Alfred Adams, who ran a shoe repair business and also had his own gymnasium where famous boxers such as Larry Gains and Charlie Colby trained.

Another character of note was the butcher, Arthur Smith, who was presented with a clock in 1923 for services rendered to Essex Police in foiling a bank raid. He apparently took his shotgun to the bank and arrested the raider on sight!

In the 1930s more street frontage was opened in the bypass (by now known as Kingsway in honour of the sovereign) and a row of shops known as 'Kingsway Parade' was built on the southern side of the road between the churchyard and the *Crown*. The *Crown* itself had taken advantage of the increased traffic being brought by the new road and had turned itself around so that the front entrance was now to the bypass rather than to the High Street.

Opposite the pub was another new attraction— the Kingsway Cinema, which opened in 1936 with a film called *Jack of All Trades*, starring Jack Hulbert. Like the

132 A clock presented to butcher, Arthur Smith, for his help in foiling a Hadleigh bank raid. The inscription reads 'Essex County Constabulary: presented to Mr. Arthur Robert Smith for assistance rendered on 20th January 1923'.

Kingsway Parade it was built by Mrs. Stanton Rolls. It was a large, imposing building, with seating for 1,500, and was described as 'the most splendid place of entertainment for miles around'. For a time it was part of the ABC chain but by the 1960s it was being run as an independent, presenting wrestling and pop music alongside films. It closed in 1970 and its site was developed as a supermarket.

West of the cinema there was still a remnant of the old *Crown* meadow, which was also used as a place of entertainment, hosting travelling fairs, circuses, boxing matches, fireworks displays and, on Boxing Day, an annual comic football match. The Public Hall (now Essex Carpets) also showed films, as well as holding revues and social events. Another local entertainment venue was the Institute, where sports such as billiards and darts could be played.

The Church

Hadleigh church, bordered by fields on the north-west since time immemorial, now found itself at the heart of the village's new road system. Hadleigh Corner had for centuries been the centre of village life, but the new road which enclosed the church into an island served even more to accentuate the focus.

With a new community growing around it, the Church itself had also to grow. This was accomplished initially by a physical extension to the hitherto largely unaltered Norman building in the form of a new vestry on the north side, built in 1928 to the designs of Sir Charles Nicholson (junior) and originally envisaged as part of a scheme for incorporating the entire church into a much larger building of which it would form only the chancel. The temptation for such massive expansion was, however, resisted and it was decided instead to build a brand new church in the centre of the growing residential area to the east of the village. A site on the corner of Church Road and Woodfield Road was acquired and the mission church of St Barnabas was erected there in the mid-1930s. This was replaced by a more modern building in the early 1960s, the tower of which is a distinctive local landmark. In the clergy, Reverend Adamson was succeeded in 1925 by Alfred Dendy, and Dendy eight years later by Leslie Stanford.

Changes were also taking place in other churches. The little Methodist chapel was struggling to meet the needs of its growing congregation and a new church was opened in 1929, at the entrance to Chapel Lane, on land largely purchased from the Salvation Army. The old chapel was taken over by James Attwood for his photographic business.

133 The Kingsway Cinema, once a grand and imposing building, is shown here shortly before its demolition in the early 1970s to make way for a new Safeway supermarket. The site is now part of a car showroom and Safeway itself has moved to new premises a few hundred yards to the west.

134 The Public Hall—popular social venue and sometime cinema. It survives today as Essex Carpets. The open space on the left is now occupied by the Hadleigh Business Centre.

135 The Broadway/ Meadow Road junction *c.*1920s, showing the Public Hall (the tall building in the centre) and adjacent businesses. The garage and Clarke's shop have now been replaced by Sketchley's.

136　The London Road, looking east towards central Hadleigh from the Chapel Lane junction. The building on the left is the *Waggon & Horses*. The houses beyond have disappeared under Safeway's carpark.

The 1920s also saw the arrival of two other churches. In 1923 an Elim Pentecostal Church was erected in Oak Road South and in 1926 a Baptist Church opened at Beresford Gardens. Meetings of both had already been taking place in local houses.

The Emergency Services

The First World War had prompted the creation of a Voluntary Fire Service but this was now inadequate for the growing village. In the 1920s the parish council acquired several sheds for the storage of brigade equipment, one of which is thought to have been behind Richardson's long-established but recently closed electrical shop in London Road.

By 1925 the council was actively looking for a proper fire station and considered buying land in Endway or taking over the old Church School. That year the still voluntary brigade joined the National Fire Brigade Association and started to look more seriously at the sort of fire-fighting equipment that was available.

There were still some outstanding issues, however, and in 1927 all but three of the firemen re-signed, apparently in a dispute over equipment. The parish council was forced to form itself into a temporary brigade, with David Stibbards, the council chairman, taking over as second officer. A new

brigade was quickly formed and a 'mile of pennies' event was organised to raise much-needed funds.

By the end of the 1920s the parish council was looking to replace the maroons which called the firemen out with a new alarm system and also to buy a modern fire engine and house it in a purpose-built station, but a decision on these issues had to wait while the discussions about the formation of Benfleet Urban District Council were being concluded.

By 1931 the new Council had settled on a site at the western end of the island formed by the new bypass and at last a proper fire station could be erected. In 1941 the brigade was incorporated into the National Fire Service and later became part of a newly-constituted County Brigade. The fire station still stands on the same site, but has been substantially modernised and enlarged.

The main issue affecting the police in the village in the 1920s was the perceived need for its two constables to be on the phone. The parish council wrote to the Chief Constable about it and was most surprised to be told that 'it is not considered desirable for police constables to have telephones installed in their private houses'. They later received a more satisfactory response that the Chief Constable was considering putting a sergeant in the village

137 Hadleigh firemen and women outside the fire station in London Road in 1943. By this stage the brigade had been incorporated into the National Fire Service, as can be seen from the alteration above the door to the original 'Benfleet U.D.C. [Urban District Council]' nameplate. The Kingsway cinema can be seen in the background to the left of the picture.

138 1935 Jubilee celebrations.

and, if that happened, he would be given a phone. Happily for the villagers it did happen and by January 1929 the situation was resolved. By the 1930s the village had its first proper police station, in Hall Crescent. One of the best remembered Hadleigh policemen from this era was PC Fred Joslin who, amongst other things, 'was well-known to youthful miscreants'!

In 1922 a hand ambulance was procured for the parish by public subscription. Mr. Yeaxlee, the draper, provided an air pillow and the kit was stored with the fire equipment. By the early 1930s a county ambulance service was in operation so there was no need for a separate local provision. An ambulance was, however, kept at the fire station during the Second World War.

Dr. Grant had been acting as surgeon for the fire brigade since 1925 and one of the best-remembered practices in the village also had its origins in this inter-war period: Dr. William James lived in Hadleigh Hall and set up a practice there with Dr. Samuel McGladdery which continued well after the war. Dr. James was later killed in a flying accident in Jersey, but Dr. McGladdery continued to run the

practice into the 1960s when it was transferred to its current site at The Hollies in Rectory Road.

The inter-war period also saw the formation of a Community Council and the construction of a County Council Health Centre.

The Early Years of the Urban District

The early years of the Urban District saw some quick returns for Hadleigh, but the bypass was still giving problems. In 1935 a 30mph speed limit was introduced through the village to try to address this.

In the first few years of its existence the Council held its meetings alternately in schools in the three parishes which it had taken over, but by the mid-1930s it was looking for land for purpose-built offices. Amongst the sites considered was Hadleigh's War Memorial Recreation Ground, though fortunately this proposal was rejected and the Council ultimately found a more suitable site in Kiln Road, Thundersley.

The late 1930s also saw a closer geographical linking of Hadleigh with South Benfleet, with the opening of Essex Way giving more direct road access to the latter village and replacing the centuries-old, much longer, route via Vicarage Hill.

139 The second of two marvellous pictures of the Salvation Army's entries for the pageant celebrating the Silver Jubilee of King George V in 1935. The themes of the waggons are 'Brickmaking Today' (138) and 'The Colony's Horticulture' (139).

140 John H. Burrows—mayor of Southend, Essex county councillor and JP—who lived at Solbys.

There were several important events for the new Council in the 1930s, with the Silver Jubilee for King George V and the Coronation celebrations for King George VI. The Silver Jubilee in 1935 included a programme of sports for children and a pageant featuring several Hadleigh organisations. The Salvation Army band played and a tea for children was held in the Army dining hall. The Coronation in 1937 took a similar form, involving organisations such as Hadleigh Ratepayers' Association, Hadleigh & District Motor Cycle & Light Car Club and the Hadleigh & Thundersley Branch of the British Legion. A bonfire was held at the castle and the church was floodlit by the Gas, Light & Coke Company (Grays & Tilbury's successors), but several other events had to be called off due to extremely inclement weather.

John H. Burrows

One of the most important local events of the 1930s was a sad one—the funeral of Alderman John H. Burrows, who died in 1935.

Burrows, who lived at Solbys, had been chairman of Essex County Council, Mayor of Southend

141 The 1935 funeral cortège of John H. Burrows, pictured in London Road to the east of the church on its way to Southend. Howard's Dairies, a well-remembered Hadleigh business, can be seen on the right. This area is now largely occupied by car showrooms.

142 Hadleigh Home Guard, whose members included Billy Welsh, Eddie Jeanes and, the officer-in-charge, Major Daniels (the first three on the left in the front row respectively). Eddie Jeanes was the son of Hadleigh parish councillor, Eli.

143 Bomb damage in Kingsway Parade, a row of shops occupied by the army during the war. Hadleigh was hit by several bombs as it lay under the flightpath for enemy bombers heading for London.

144 The small garden to the west of the Salvation Army Temple used to be the village horsepond. Carts could be driven down into the pond to enable horses to drink from it. This picture dates from *c.*1940 when it was enlarged to provide a better source of water for combatting fires caused by enemy bombing. Note the large number of firemen involved with the building work, all under the direction of Mr. Dodd (standing on the rubble). The canvas bag on the left was usually filled with water and used for fire practices. The pond was later stocked with fish.

and a JP and had given almost half a century of public service to Essex people. He was particularly interested in education and health issues and was chairman of Messrs John H. Burrows & Sons Ltd., proprietors of *The Southend Standard* newspaper.

A native of Dublin, Burrows had come to southeast Essex in 1882 at the age of 28, initially living in Southend but moving to Solbys in 1905. He had performed the unveiling ceremony at Hadleigh war memorial, given over a field in front of Solbys for use by the Thundersley & Hadleigh cricket club and lent his support to the old parish council on numerous occasions.

The funeral took the form of a short service at Solbys followed by a procession through the streets from Hadleigh to Prittlewell church where a full service took place before the final leg of the journey to Sutton Road Cemetery. An obituary in the press recalled that 'Mr. Burrow's public utterances bore the hallmark of sincerity and, however much his opponents might differ from his views, his personal integrity was never in question'.

In 1936 the Urban District Council decided to purchase Solbys for use as a museum and put its grounds to use as a recreation amenity for the people of the district, naming it the John H. Burrows Recreation Ground in honour of the man who had lived there. The museum never materialised, but the recreation ground, since extended, has proved a valuable amenity for Hadleigh people.

The Second World War

The period of rapid development which had dominated the 1920s and 1930s was brought to a close by the onset of war. The Urban District Council had set up an Air Raid Precautions Committee as early as 1935 and once the war was officially underway the whole district soon found itself on the enemy flightpath to London.

A Parish (Invasion) Sub-committee was formed to oversee civil defences and yet more fire brigade cover was provided as Hadleigh geared up to face the expected onslaught. Air-raid shelters were built behind the shops on the north side of the bypass

145 In a time of strict food rationing, the arrival of bananas at Owen's greengrocers was a cause for celebration amongst Hadleigh shoppers. One pound of bananas was allowed per ration book and villagers were evidently quick to make the most of their allowance.

(where the carpark is now) and on open ground north of The Broadway near the Council School. Schoolchildren had lessons in the latter on some occasions. The newly opened John H. Burrows Recreation Ground and the shops on the south side of the bypass were both taken over by the army.

South of the village a large area of the Downs in the vicinity of Sayers Farm was requisitioned by the military and anti-aircraft guns were placed there to work in tandem with weapons on the Kent side to shoot down aircraft flying up the Thames. They were manned by Royal Artillery units, including one from the Essex Regiment. Weapons included four 3in. guns of a First World War naval type, though these were later supplemented by 3.7in. and 4.5in. guns. The Downs were used for military manoeuvres and training exercises and a searchlight was erected on Plumtree Hill to pick out targets for the guns to shoot down. The main army area south of Sayers Farm became almost a complete, self-contained community with its own water supply

146 One of several Victory Parties which took place in Hadleigh streets at the end of the war. This one is thought to have been in The Crescent.

and sewerage system and guards at the entrance to keep out unwanted visitors. Vibration caused by the guns sometimes broke the windows of houses in the village. The Royal Signals Corp also had a base there, training carrier pigeons on the Downs for work in France to convey messages from the Resistance to the Allies.

Hadleigh was filled with soldiers throughout much of the war: on the Downs, in the bypass shops and in a house called St Mary's in Hadleigh High Street, which was at one time occupied by the Home Guard. They were also billeted in some local homes. Farm carts were used to block main road access to Southend (which was a restricted area) and explosives were laid across Castle Lane in case of invasion from a landing near the castle. Fields and ditches around the eastern end of Scrub Lane were also put to military use, with guns and vehicles being hidden under the trees. Events for soldiers were held at places such as the Methodist Church and the Public Hall. Highlands, Queens, Manchester and King's Own Light Yeomanry troops were all represented, whilst down in the waters below the village ships were gathering for the Normandy invasion. The river was a hive of activity until one day in June 1944, when the ships were suddenly gone.

Despite all the precautions some bombs inevitably fell on Hadleigh, landing amongst other places in Kingsway and Park Chase and in the vicinity of the Salvation Army Temple and St Barnabas' church.

When the war was over street parties were held throughout the village and the war memorial in the Recreation Ground was updated to commemorate the actions of those who had fought for their country. The military eventually withdrew from the John H. Burrows Recreation Ground and the air-raid shelters were demolished. The foundations of the guns in Chapel Lane were covered over by spoil, but the humps formed by their positions can still be seen.

The war had caused another pause in Hadleigh's development, but what would the post-war period bring?

CHAPTER IX

Modern Hadleigh

After the war, Hadleigh settled down to a modern way of life. The backwater village of yesteryear was now a world away and Hadleigh had virtually become a suburb of Southend. Nevertheless, it managed to retain its independence, thanks in part to the protection offered by the surrounding woodland and farmland which acted as a buffer zone for development. New estates still cropped up, but a growing environmental awareness ensured that they were largely restricted to infill developments rather than being built on areas of open space.

Two notable building projects which did take place in the early years after the war were the construction of council houses in Seymour Road and the repair of the church roof, which had been damaged by enemy action. The repairs were completed in 1949 and a full reopening ceremony took place, overseen by the Bishop of Chelmsford.

On the Downs there was some contention over the future of Hadleigh Castle, which was taken into the care of the Ministry of Works in 1948 and for access to which the Ministry now proposed to charge a fee. A petition was organised, objecting to the Ministry's proposals and expressing the view that access to the castle had been free since time immemorial and villagers did not intend to pay for it now. The Ministry relented and entry to the castle remains free to this day.

In 1953 the coronation of Queen Elizabeth II gave villagers cause for celebration and street parties were held in some roads. Local schoolchildren were

147 Church roof repairs.

148 A close-up of the repairs to the church roof which were carried out in 1949.

149 The High Street in 1949, looking towards Hadleigh Hall. After centuries as the main street of Hadleigh village, the High Street as a shopping centre began to decline after the war as businesses moved in greater numbers to the London Road/Kingsway bypass. This scene is now totally altered.

150 The *Crown* from the London Road/Kingsway bypass, showing Reynold's scrapyard in the High Street beyond. This picture was taken in 1949 when the cottages where the library now stands (far right) were still there.

151 By the late 1940s the 1924 bypass—usually by now referred to as Kingsway or the London Road—had become a busy shopping street in its own right. The Kingsway Parade (shown here) was occupied during the war by soldiers; after the war, the shop on the right did a roaring trade in army surplus stock. The car lot in the centre of the picture is still used for car sales, but the vehicles have changed a bit since this photo was taken!

given a suitably inscribed book about Royalty in Essex to commemorate the event.

The High Street

As the 1950s opened and developed, the future of the old High Street as a shopping area began to look bleak. Businesses such as Dossett's bakery soldiered on, but the shift of business from the High Street to the bypass which had begun before the war was rapidly accelerating and the High Street began to decline. Even Yeaxlee's new bypass business was destined for change—later becoming Thomas's.

One of the most conspicuous businesses in the High Street at this period was Reynold's scrapyard, which was stacked high with items in such an apparently higgledy-piggledy way that residents could never understand how anything was found! It would periodically change its topography as items came and went, as if undergoing some kind of magical metamorphosis.

By the time of the Essex Development Plan (Report on the First Review) in 1964 it was recorded that 'the majority of the premises [in the High Street] are in an apparently poor condition and the shopping frontage is broken by residential, storage and industrial uses'.

Post-war Traffic

For a long time after the war traffic remained two-way on both roads in the village. The old parish council's request for a one-way system still went unheeded and, with more and more motor traffic replacing the traditional horse and cart, there were frequent accidents where the two roads met.

Tourists heading for Southend often took the wrong route (through the old High Street) and a sign was erected pointing them the safer way along the bypass. Accidents still occurred with alarming regularity, however, and local residents who lived in the vicinity of the fire station were given bandages by the Red Cross with which they could treat injured drivers if the emergency services were late arriving on the scene!

Concerns were also growing about the increasing number of accidents to the west of the village at

Victoria House Corner (which still took the form of a staggered crossroads) and a report was presented to the Urban District Council.

In 1948 Essex County Council made an application to the Ministry of Transport to introduce some improvements to the London Road. Their proposals included a remarkable plan for the construction of 'a 100ft spur road through the centre of the allotments and recreation ground at Hadleigh'. Nothing came of this scheme and it would be several years before any major changes were made.

The 1953 Flood

Perhaps the most significant event in the locality in the 1950s was the 'Great Tide' of 1953 which made national headlines as it swept down the east coast overnight on 31 January, making thousands homeless and claiming several lives. One of the greatest centres of destruction was on Canvey Island, which was completely flooded.

As the day broke on 1 February the full horror of what had happened began to dawn. The marshes below the castle were flooded and water stretched right across to Kent, with only the roofs of flooded houses on Canvey breaking the surface. Several Hadleigh people went immediately to assist the relief operation, including local fire crews, police

officers, doctors and other public-spirited individuals. The fire crews also helped out at Wallasea Island near Rochford and at Pitsea Marshes, which were also flooded.

Local schools, including Hadleigh primary (the former Council School) in Church Road, were opened to receive flood victims and helpers set about providing hot meals and warm blankets for those seeking shelter. Many of the blankets at the school were supplied by the Salvation Army, who also gave much practical and spiritual assistance to the distraught victims.

Parents and friends of the school also lent a hand as buses full of tired and exhausted Canvey inhabitants arrived in the village and soup was obtained from a local cafe. Some 900 Canvey people passed through Hadleigh primary in the days after the flood, with as many as 350 sleeping there overnight. Hadleigh fire station was used as a rest centre for exhausted firemen from several local stations, while the Salvation Army used their sheds and pens to house homeless families' equally homeless pets.

One of the other schools in the area which received flood victims was a new one—a secondary school in Benfleet Road which was scheduled to open within days of the flood. The opening was, not surprisingly, postponed. Originally known as

152   An aerial photograph of what is now the King John School, taken during the 1950s. Even before it opened the school played a vital community role, being used as a receiving centre for flood victims from Canvey Island during the Great Tide of 1953.

153   The new library, built on the site of the cottages in picture 150 and opened in 1963.

Benfleet Secondary Modern, the school would eventually become the King John School and would take many of its pupils from the Hadleigh area.

The 1960s

The 1960s was to prove another boom period for Hadleigh and the rate of this growth is captured by the 1964 Essex Development Plan (Report on the First Review). A survey of the District in 1949-1952 (reported in 1957) had estimated a provisional population for Benfleet, Hadleigh and Thundersley of 35,000 in 1971. By the time of the 1964 report, however, the population was already up to 32,400 (from 19,570 in 1951).

Benfleet, Hadleigh and Thundersley were prime targets for development, with property being marketed to commuters who found access to London via Benfleet station and a home in comparatively rural south-east Essex a perfect combination. The electrification of the railway line in 1962 and improvements to the platform and crossing arrangements at Benfleet served only to make the idea even more attractive.

The Falboro Crescent/Westwood Gardens and Sherwood Crescent areas were developed around this period and most of the remaining unfilled gaps to the east of the village towards the Highlands Estate were plugged. This included the development of an area variously known as Grant's Farm and

Greenacres which was a smallholding used in conjunction with Dossett's bakery for the breeding of pigs for their prize-winning pork pies. The smallholding was run by Joe Grant and a large pond nearby became known as Grant's Pond. Originally centred around a bungalow called Resthaven, the site of the smallholding is now approximately where Greenacres road is. Resthaven was said to have once been used as a convent and to have later had a curse put on it. Several epidemics of swine fever on the smallholding may well have owed their origins to this curse. The smallholding was sold out of the family in 1951 and, when the area was developed, Scrub Lane, still a muddy track, was made up. Dossett's shop closed in 1982 after at least 60 years of service.

Some new bungalows were also erected in Florence Gardens in the 1960s, the contract going to a well-known local building firm, Wiggins & Sons.

In the centre of Hadleigh, the Post Office moved from the High Street to a new site in Rectory Road and a new library appeared. The library, built on the site of some High Street cottages which had once housed Batchelor's bakery, had previously been temporarily housed in several local buildings, including schools and churches, plus a site on the corner of Church Road, so purpose-built premises were long overdue. They opened in 1963.

154 St Barnabas' Church at the junction of Church Road and Woodfield Road. It began as a mission hall in the 1930s for the growing residential area between Hadleigh and Leigh. The current building was opened in the early 1960s and its tower is now a distinctive local landmark.

Amongst the other amenities provided at this time were two new primary schools in Bilton Road and Beresford Gardens. The Bilton Road site became Hadleigh County Infants School (now the infants and nursery school), freeing up space at the old Council School in Church Road to enable that to concentrate on junior-age pupils as Hadleigh County Junior School. The Beresford Gardens school took the name Westwood County Primary. The school situation had been desperate for some years—in 1949,

450 secondary school pupils throughout the Urban District had had to be taught in primary schools because there was just not the accommodation available. With this in mind, a secondary school site was also earmarked and this, when opened in the early 1970s as the Deanes School (off Rayleigh Road, Thundersley), would operate in tandem with the King John School in Benfleet Road.

The schooling situation was not the only one giving problems. Planners expressed their concern

155 The 1929 Methodist Church, expanded in the 1960s to incorporate a new youth hall.

that there was no central shopping area for the Urban District and that the one at Hadleigh, though well appointed, was rather dangerous because through-traffic and pedestrians continually mixed. In order to address some of the safety issues it was decided to try to curtail the eastward sprawl of the main shopping area (towards the Salvation Army field) and to introduce off-road parking on a new site off Rectory Road. Better crossing arrangements were also introduced.

The road itself—that old bane of the local council—was still proving too congested and the County began seriously to look at viable options for improvement. They finally adopted the old parish council's idea of a one-way system and, eventually, set in train the process of converting the staggered crossroads at Victoria House Corner into a roundabout. This roundabout was later enlarged and the section from there to the fire station was turned into a dual-carriageway.

A much grander scheme was also proposed—a new road connecting the Tarpots area of Benfleet with Southend along the marshes below the castle. The scheme as originally envisaged was never completed, but a new road off Canvey Island to Sadler's Farm in Benfleet subsequently fulfilled part of the dream. The other part—the road across the marshes to Southend—has periodically raised its head, but has each time been rejected for environmental reasons.

The introduction of the one-way system and its associated road-widening led to the demolition of some old cottages which had stood in the High Street to the south of the church for several centuries (though one had already been destroyed by fire). The opportunity was taken in 1968 to excavate this site and several interesting finds were made, including traces of medieval buildings, pottery sherds and evidence of a ditch with ramparts.

Another major demolition at this time was that in 1961 of Hadleigh Hall, which was replaced by a parade of shops that incorporated Wallis'—Hadleigh's first supermarket. A large notice was erected outside the Hall, advertising its doors, windows and timbers for 'demolition salvage' or firewood. Barely a few years earlier the Hall had been considered as a site for the new library, in which role it would have rivalled nearby Leigh-on-Sea's 'old rectory' library for atmosphere and history.

The name 'Hadleigh Hall' did not completely disappear, however, as it has since been given to a community building at the John H. Burrows Recreation Ground. There, the old mansion of Solbys saw some changes of its own, with its conversion into private flats for the elderly.

Other old properties consigned to the rubbish dump of history during the post-war development boom included Scrub House, which disappeared under housing, and Reverend Thomas Espin's 1856

156   Safeway's new supermarket, opened in 1982 and now the focal point of Hadleigh shopping.

rectory, which was replaced by a new, smaller rectory and a new road, Rectory Close.

The Church

The church, too, had some modern changes. A new organ and balcony were erected in 1968, followed four years later by the introduction of some ancient paving stones to the altar area after their discovery underneath the floor. In 1985 the vestry was enlarged to provide kitchen and toilet facilities. Roger Lewis, John Hughes, Athelstan John Morley and Michael Ketley are the men who have ministered here in this modern era.

The Methodist Church continued to expand and a new Youth Hall was opened next to the main building in 1962. Like the nearby bungalows in Florence Gardens, it was built by the local firm, Wiggins & Sons.

The Congregational Church—now the United Reformed Church following a national merger with the Presbyterians—was also enlarged and modernised, whilst in 1982 the newest of Hadleigh's mainstream churches—the Roman Catholic Church of St Thomas More—was erected.

The Last 30 Years

The years since the 1960s have seen many changes, but not on the scale of the developments which took place then or in the inter-war period.

The gradual decline of the Salvation Army Colony towards the end of the 1960s saw several planning applications submitted for new housing developments on the northern fringes of Army property, but virtually all of these were turned down. The small Florence Gardens development was supplemented in the 1980s by the new roads of Mountnessing and Galleydene and an extension to nearby Homestead Gardens/Sandbanks. Odd infills of small sites have taken place—such as the King's and Queen's Lodge flats at Victoria House Corner—but no spectacular new estates have emerged to transform the seemingly ever-changing Hadleigh landscape.

In 1974 local government reorganisation brought an end to the 45-year reign of the Benfleet Urban District Council and amalgamated it with Canvey Island Urban District Council to form the new Castle Point District. Named from Canvey's low-lying Point area and Hadleigh's hilltop castle, the district prospered and in 1992 was elevated to Borough status. Amongst the Urban District Council's final acts were the twinning of the district with Romainville in France and Lovenich (now Cologne District 3) in Germany.

The biggest development on the shopping front in Hadleigh in recent years was the opening in 1982 of Safeway's supermarket on land that once formed part of the old *Crown* meadow. This replaced their old supermarket which had been developed in the 1970s on the site of the Kingsway Cinema. Safeway's soon became the shopping focal point of the village, following the closure of other supermarkets such as Wallis', Co-op and International which had appeared in the 1960s and 1970s.

The nearby *Waggon & Horses* suffered a major fire during this period, which made headline news and led to it requiring substantial rebuilding.

Today

In 1991 the population of the whole of Castle Point Borough was over 85,000. The figure for the old Hadleigh parish alone (approximately the area covered by St James and Victoria wards under the new authority [including Daws Heath and a little bit of Thundersley]) was over 11,000—a far cry from the 526 souls who had lived there only a century earlier.

The main issue in the village today is probably still the traffic. The dual-carriageway to the west of the fire station and the single-carriageway to the east of the church have meant that cars funnel through the village at an alarming rate, only to meet stationary vehicles at the other end.

Apart from the ever-increasing through-traffic, Hadleigh has become something of a mecca for car showrooms, particularly in the old Broadway area to the east of the church. Cars and shoppers seem to be continually in conflict, with the bus lane in the Southend-bound carriageway a particular danger.

One of the most contentious issues in recent years was the plan in 1997 to close Hadleigh fire station, which generated massive opposition throughout the area. With three appliances and an average of 48 men, Hadleigh's is a busy station, serving a large area of south-east Essex and often covering other stations when their vehicles are unavailable. A stay of execution was secured by protesters, but for how long?

To the outsider, Hadleigh has lost something of its identity as a clearly defined community, being somewhat swallowed up in the urban sprawl that connects Benfleet to Southend. Certainly, it can no longer really be described as a village, but it does have a distinct centre and the church, as always, remains its focal point.

Despite all its changes and the massive development which has taken place in certain areas of the parish, Hadleigh still retains much of its natural landscape, both on the Downs around the castle and in the ancient woodland in the north of the parish. This natural open space provides one of the best amenities for the residents of the otherwise built-up south-east Essex area, not least through one of its newest natural attractions, Hadleigh Castle Country Park.

CHAPTER X

The Woodland, the Nature Reserve and the Country Park

The country park is just one of Hadleigh's many natural attractions. The woods that curved around the north of the village in 1777 have survived largely intact and even the old Royal Parkland has been spared the developer's attentions. Hadleigh has consequently become something of a mecca for recreation in this otherwise crowded corner of south-east Essex.

Woodland History

For a county that was once thickly wooded, Essex retains comparatively little of its original ancient tree cover. This woodland, often referred to as the 'wildwood', has been gradually destroyed over the centuries for agriculture and, more recently, housing. Even in 1086 Essex was probably down to about 20 per cent woodland—and even less in the south-eastern corner. By 1768 the Essex historian, Philip Morant, was lamenting the loss of woodland in the old Rochford Hundred area (which included Hadleigh), but losses at this stage were comparatively minor—there was no wholesale destruction like that which took place in the early 19th century. By 1827, another observer would record with sorrow that 'the woods behind Hadley Turnpike are now converted into cornfields'.

The unrelenting demands of agriculture and development have led to the destruction of several

157 An early view of Hadleigh woodland.

158 Hadleigh Great Wood, *c*.1930—shortly before its designation as a nature reserve.

Hadleigh woods over the years. These include: Solbys or Coxall Wood, which stood between Poors Lane and Daws Heath Road and which was destroyed after the war for housing; Horseleigh Wood, also lost to housing from the 1920s onwards and which stood in the vicinity of the northern end of Woodfield Road; and Luther's Wood, a small, partly re-grown wood at the northern end of Poors Lane. Certain adjacent woods in Leigh-on-Sea have also been destroyed.

Hadleigh, it will be remembered, is named from its location as a heath clearing within the once-extensive forest which covered Essex and, despite the destruction, many of the best examples of ancient woodland in this corner of the county survive both here and at nearby Hockley.

According to the *Victoria County History of Essex* 'the finest stretches of woodland in the county, next to those of Epping Forest, are the Highwoods at

159 The Poors Lane entrance to Hadleigh Great Wood, which was saved from destruction by a campaign in the 1930s.

Writtle and the Hadleigh Great Wood and Hockley Wood in Rochford Hundred'. Some of the individual Hadleigh woods are therefore worth a closer look.

Belfairs Nature Reserve

Hadleigh Great Wood (anciently called Barnes Wood) and neighbouring Dodd's Grove are now better known as 'Belfairs Nature Reserve'. Both were formerly owned by the Dean and Chapter of St Paul's, before passing into the ownership of the Ecclesiastical Commissioners. By the early 1920s they were in private ownership and, with land to the south being developed for housing, there was serious concern they would be swallowed up by development.

By 1934 sufficient concern was being expressed for the formation of a South Essex Natural History Society, under the auspices of Dr. George Stovin and Henry Huggins, both eminent entomologists. The society's inaugural meeting resolved to investigate transforming the remaining woodland into a nature reserve and thus began a four-year campaign to further that aim.

Campaigners, led by Dr. Stovin, had the support of the local press (one of the sons of John H. Burrows was a society member) as well as the backing of several important national organisations. They immediately set about trying to get the local authorities to purchase the land for public use. Hadleigh headmaster, Henry Reginald Tutt, a member of Benfleet Urban District Council and a keen ornithologist, did much to persuade his colleagues at the council (and at Southend Borough and Essex County Councils, who were being asked to contribute financially) to consider the benefits of creating a reserve.

By 1938 sufficient support, including a petition of over 20,000 names, had been gained to convince the authorities that the land should be purchased for the intended purpose. Surprisingly, Southend Council met most of the cost, although the land was technically in Benfleet Urban District. By 1947 Dodd's Grove had been acquired and the reserve largely took on its current shape. 'Belfairs Nature Reserve', as the whole area became known, was the first of its kind in Essex.

Today the reserve covers over 90 acres and is a popular recreational area and invaluable educational resource. It is formally designated a Local Nature Reserve and a Site of Special Scientific Interest and is regarded as one of the best examples of ancient woodland in south-east Essex. In 1998 a series of events was held to mark its 60th anniversary.

The nature reserve is contiguous to another ancient wood called Belfairs Wood (most of which is in Leigh-on-Sea). This is an area which has not enjoyed the protection of nature reserve status and it has consequently suffered some damage from dogs and horseriding. It has also, as one writer put it, 'suffered the comic fate' of being preserved by having a golf course bulldozed through it. Nevertheless, with the accompanying public park, it too provides a valuable recreational amenity in the Hadleigh locality.

West Wood

West Wood, once the property of the Dean and Chapter of St Paul's, is now in the ownership of the

160   The Rayleigh Road entrance to West Wood, operated by Castle Point Borough Council on lease from the Church Commissioners.

161   Pound Wood, seen here from the St Michael's Road entrance.

Church Commissioners but is leased to Castle Point Borough Council as a recreational amenity for local people.

It straddles the boundary with neighbouring Thundersley parish and, following rapid growth in the area, has also suffered some destruction. Nevertheless, it contains several ancient features, such as Saxon woodbanks and pollarded oaks, which once marked the boundaries of separate woodland ownerships.

It covers approximately 80 acres and, like the Great Wood, has probably, by a curious irony, been saved from destruction by being turned into a public amenity.

Pound Wood

Like West Wood, Pound Wood straddles the parish boundary with Thundersley, but it has been less visited because it has not been publicly accessible for so long and is, in any case, more remote from local population.

Most of it is ancient woodland, dating back to at least medieval times and formerly in the ownership of the Dean and Chapter of Westminster. There is a woodbank from the early medieval period and the wood was anciently a source of fence poles and

firewood, as the not-too-distant *Woodman's Arms* pub in Thundersley recalls.

Since 1993 Pound Wood has been owned by the Essex Wildlife Trust and is actively managed to encourage a wider range of flowering plants and associated wildlife. Part of the wood is a non-intervention area, protected from human interference. The whole wood covers just over 50 acres.

Hadleigh Castle Country Park

Arguably the most important recreational amenity in Hadleigh is Hadleigh Castle Country Park.

The park takes the form of three distinct areas, covering 475 acres in total and stretching from Belton Hills and Two Tree Island in Leigh to the Downs in Benfleet (its largest part). A seawall walk and a footpath over the Saddleback (past the castle) connect Two Tree Island and Belton Hills respectively with the Benfleet part of the park. The public open space around the castle and the open farmland of the Salvation Army's Home Farm make the whole area one of the most open and attractive in south-east Essex.

The idea of a country park arose in the 1930s when the environmentally conscious Benfleet Urban

162 The information board and gate at the Chapel Lane entrance to Hadleigh Castle Country Park.

District Council took up a suggestion to purchase an area of Benfleet Downs for use as public open space. This was opened in 1934 by Sir Edgar Bonham Carter, chairman of the Open Spaces Preservation Society, and was envisaged as the first phase of a 'regional park' which would stretch from Benfleet to Leigh.

The impetus for further expansion was not, however, provided until the Countryside Act of 1968, which empowered local authorities to establish country parks to 'provide opportunities for enjoyment of the countryside'. The Essex Development Plan report of 1964 had identified the establishment of a country park as one of the main local needs for the Urban District and by 1971 Essex County Council had issued a draft scheme consultation plan presenting various options for the use of the Downs. The draft scheme included several formal sporting activities which were never developed, such as cricket pitches, a golf course and a boating lake. One sport did take place—motorcycle scrambling—which proved to be a popular weekend attraction.

From the outset the neighbouring local authorities worked closely with one another to examine the potential of a country park and a Joint Steering Committee comprising representatives from Essex County, Benfleet Urban District, Canvey Island Urban District and Southend County Borough Councils was established under the chairmanship of Councillor W.R. Marrison, a member of both the County Planning Committee and Benfleet Urban District Council. The park was expected to serve 750,000 people, providing a valuable lung of recreational land in an otherwise largely built-up area.

As proposals were considered and rejected, time dragged on. In 1973 a Public Inquiry was held, ultimately finding in favour of establishing a park from Benfleet to Leigh, but it was to be another 14 years before the dream could become reality. The official opening of the park took place on 18 May 1987 when 458 acres were unveiled. Two old farms, Poynetts and Kersey (both in Benfleet), form a substantial part of the new parkland and the park's name is still a little misleading since neither the castle, nor much of Hadleigh, lie within it.

Negotiations have periodically taken place about the acquisition of additional land, as much of the original area identified for inclusion is still owned by the Salvation Army. Some land exchanges have taken

163 Visitors stream through the gates of Hadleigh Castle Country Park on 18 May 1987, the day of its formal opening.

place (such as that allowing carparking and access at the bottom of Chapel Lane), but there is still a long way to go before the full extent of the park as originally envisaged can be realised.

Planning applications, notably a refused and highly controversial application for the development of the Salvation Army field on the London Road to the east of Hadleigh, have also cropped up. Most of these have been for areas currently outside the park, but any development in the close vicinity would undoubtedly have a detrimental visual impact on the park itself. The only significant application so far approved has been for the Mountnessing/Galleydene lands behind Florence Gardens.

Perhaps the most controversial recent proposal was the 1991 plan to build a relief road off Canvey Island across the marshes below the castle and up to the London Road near Tattersall Gardens. This was vigorously opposed by locals on the mainland, with an initial protest meeting at Belfairs School in Leigh attracting 400 people. A 'Save Hadleigh Castle Country Park' group was formed and, after an ultimately successful campaign, this group evolved into a new permanent organisation, the Friends of Hadleigh Castle Country Park, which works alongside Essex County Council to encourage public interest in the park and safeguard its future.

The park today contains a wide range of wildlife habitats, including remnants of ancient woodland, downland, dykes and ponds, flower-rich grassland and grazing marshes and it is particularly attractive to a wide range of butterflies and moths, as well as to Brent Geese. The seawall walk offers views over the saltmarsh and mudflats—Essex's most important contribution to the global environment. Such is the park's importance that it is designated a Site of Special Scientific Interest, a Coastal Protection Zone, a Coastal Nature Conservation Zone, a Special Landscape Area and part of the Metropolitan Green Belt. Decisions about its future are still made by a Joint Committee, now comprised of representatives from Essex County, Southend Borough and Castle Point Borough Councils.

The Future

Despite extensive residential development, there remains a vast amount of undeveloped land in Hadleigh. The future of the surviving woodland areas and the designated country park should be assured and the only land of any size which could succumb to the developer is that owned by the Salvation Army. Much of this could be regarded as prime development land, but it could also be regarded as ideal for inclusion in an expanded country park.

Rather like the Ministry of Defence on nearby Foulness Island, the presence of the Salvation Army and its long concentration on agriculture has certainly helped Hadleigh retain much of its countrified feel. Whatever happens, the wonderful natural amenities provided by the district will ensure that Hadleigh remains a popular recreational area for many years to come.

Hadleigh began with a castle and a park and it seems fitting that this history should end in similar circumstances.

Select Bibliography

A Guide To Southend, by a Gentleman (1824)

Armytage, W.H.B., *Heavens Below—Utopian Experiments in England 1560-1900* (1961)

Benton, Philip, *The History of Rochford Hundred* (1867)

Booth, William, *In Darkest England—And The Way Out* (1890)

Brake, George Thompson, *The History of the Methodist Church in the Southend and Leigh Circuit—Hadleigh* (1994)

Burrows, John W., *Southend-on-Sea & District: Historical Notes* (1909)

Dilley, Roy, *The Dream Palaces of Southend* (1984)

Drewett, P.L., *Excavations at Hadleigh Castle, Essex, 1971-2* (1975)

Ellis, Clarence, *Hubert De Burgh—A Study In Constancy* (1952)

Essex Record Office Library, *John Henry Burrows 1854-1935—A Memoir* (c.1935)

Fairbank, Jenty, *Booth's Boots* (1983)

Gifford, P.R. (ed.), *Resist the Invader* (1982)

Grieve, Hilda, *The Great Tide* (1953)

Haggard, H. Rider, *The Poor & The Land* (1905)

Haggard, H. Rider, *Redemption* (1910)

Hancock, M. and Harvey, S., *Hadleigh—An Essex Village* (1986)

Heygate, W.E., *Sir Henry Appleton* (1859)

Jennings-Smith, D., *Hadleigh Castle Country Park Draft Scheme Consultation* (1971)

Maley, E.A.B., *The Ancient Parish of Thundersley, Essex* (c.1937)

Maple, Eric, *Cunning Murrell* (1960)

Morrison, Arthur, *Cunning Murrell* (1900)

Morrison, Arthur, 'A Wizard of Yesterday', *Strand Magazine* (1900)

Neale, Kenneth, *Essex Heritage* (1992)

Priestley, Harold, *A History of Benfleet—Early Days* (1977)

Priestley, Harold, *A History of Benfleet—Modern Times* (1984)

Rackham, Oliver, *The Woods of South East Essex* (1986)

Rodwell, Warwick, *South East Essex in the Roman Period* (1971)

Sandall, Robert, *The History of the Salvation Army* (1955)

Simpson, F.D. and Clark, P.F., *The Bridge Family and its Buses* (1983)

Sorrell, Mark, *The Peculiar People* (1979)

Spooner, B.M. and Bowdrey, J.P. (Ed.), *Hadleigh Great Wood* (1988)

Vidia Productions, *Cunning Murrell* (cassette), (1992)

Other Salvation Army publications: *Hadleigh—The Story of a Great Endeavour* (c.1905) and *Illustrated Guide to the Salvation Army Land & Industrial Colony* (c.1927). Magazines: *All The World*, *The Colonist*, *The Deliverer*, *The Social Gazette* and *War Cry*.

Also—guidebooks to Hadleigh castle and church, various *Transactions* of the Essex Archaeological Society, various articles in *Essex Countryside*, *Essex Journal* and local newspapers, Hadleigh parish council and parish vestry minutes, Benfleet Urban District Council minutes, *Kelly's Directories*, *Park News* (the newsletter of the Friends of Hadleigh Castle Country Park) and various documents held by the Essex Record Office.

Index

References which relate to illustrations only are given in **bold**.

The Salvation Army Industrial and Land Colony.

LEIGH PARK RECEIVING HOME, HADLEIGH, ESSEX.

PROBATIONER'S DECLARATION AND AGREEMENT.

I, the undersigned, hereby declare that in consequence of my homeless, friendless and destitute condition, or other circumstances set forth in the annexed schedule, I desire to be enrolled as a Probationer for work on the Training Farm of the Industrial and Land Colony; and I declare that the scheduled information is true in substance and in fact, and embodies all material facts affecting my past life, which I am now anxious to reform.

I therefore voluntarily agree to the following terms and conditions of admission, which I fully understand and appreciate, namely :—

1. To submit unconditionally to all the Rules and Regulations which exist now, or may hereafter be framed, *and particularly* to a thorough cleansing of the body and an examination of my clothing. If in the opinion of the Officer-in-charge the latter is considered useless, it may be destroyed or held in reserve at his discretion.

2. Whatever clothing may be deemed necessary for my work and personal comfort shall be supplied to me *on loan*, and can only become *my* property by concession, in writing, from the Governor.

3. Should I leave the Training Farm, taking such clothing with me without first obtaining a written concession, I render myself liable to prosecution for theft.

4. In the event of any breach of this agreement resulting in my having to leave, I fully understand that I shall only be entitled to the clothing which was on my person at the time of my arrival, unless I may have legitimately acquired new clothing of my own ; and should my said clothing have been destroyed, I agree to accept in substitution such garments as the Officer-in-charge thinks fit to provide me with.

5. Under no circumstances, other than set forth in Clause 2, can I claim proprietorship of any boots or wearing apparel that may have been voluntarily supplied to me as necessary to my comfort and work, neither can I prefer any claim for clothing that may have been destroyed in terms of Clause 1.

6. This agreement shall remain in force for a period of three months from the date hereof, and until the expiration of that term I will not apply for outside work, neither will I ask, or expect. other remuneration than *food and shelter* in return for my labour ; the object of this contract being to afford me an opportunity of redeeming my character, regaining strength, and eventually becoming a useful and trustworthy man.